MEDIA MADE IN CALIFORNIA

MEDIA MADE
IN
CALIFORNIA
Hollywood, Politics, and the News

JEREMY TUNSTALL

DAVID WALKER

New York   Oxford
OXFORD UNIVERSITY PRESS
1981

Copyright © 1981 by Jeremy Tunstall and David Walker

Library of Congress Cataloging in Publication Data
Tunstall, Jeremy.
Media made in California.

Bibliography: p.
1. Mass media—California. 2. California—
Popular culture. 3. California—Politics and
government—1951–   . I. Walker, David,
       1950–   joint author. II. Title.
P92.U5T78   302.2′3   80-26744
ISBN 0-19-502922-4   AACR1

*Selections from works by the following authors were made possible by the kind
permission of their respective publishers:*

Brooke Hayward: Excerpt from *Haywire*. Copyright © 1977 by Brooke
Hayward. Reprinted by permission of Alfred A. Knopf, Inc.

Irving Howe: Excerpt from *World of Our Fathers*. Copyright © 1975 by Irving
Howe. Reprinted by permission of Harcourt Brace Jovanovich, Inc.

Kenneth Tynan: Excerpt from *Show People*. Copyright © 1979 by Kenneth
Tynan. Reprinted by permission of Simon & Schuster, a Division of Gulf &
Western Corporation.

Printing (last digit): 9 8 7 6 5 4 3 2 1

Printed in the United States of America

Acknowledgments

We owe much of our information and not a few of our perspectives to people in the Californian media who generously gave us their time to talk and answer our questions. About 150 individuals in Los Angeles, San Francisco, San Diego, the Bay Area, Washington, D.C., and Sacramento collectively deserve our thanks.

In 1978–79 we both enjoyed California hospitality through the University of California. David Walker was at U.C. Berkeley, thanks to the Harkness Fellowship program; Jeremy Tunstall was visiting professor at U.C. San Diego, on leave from his London post. Numerous colleagues, neighbors, students, and library staff were helpful. Back in London the library staff of the City University has given invaluable assistance: the bibliography at the back of the book is a selective one.

Both of us learned much simply from living in the state—at two poles, Oakland and La Jolla. Karen Walker and Sylvia, Rebecca, Helena, and Paul Tunstall helped make the experience enjoyable; they did not object too strongly to being within fairly constant earshot of radio and television and submerged under piles of newspapers and magazines for a whole year. David

Walker's knowledge of American politics is better than it might have been thanks to Senator Jacob K. Javits and Representative William M. Brodhead and their staffs with whom he worked in Washington, D.C., in 1977–78.

Our gratitude goes to those who read and commented on an early draft—Kurt Lang, Herbert Gans, Herbert Schiller, and Jim Skellie. Richard Evans and Ian Drummond put David Walker right about Frank Zappa. Our agent Michael Sissons and our publisher Sheldon Meyer were all that mentors should be.

London   J.T.
October 1980   D.W.

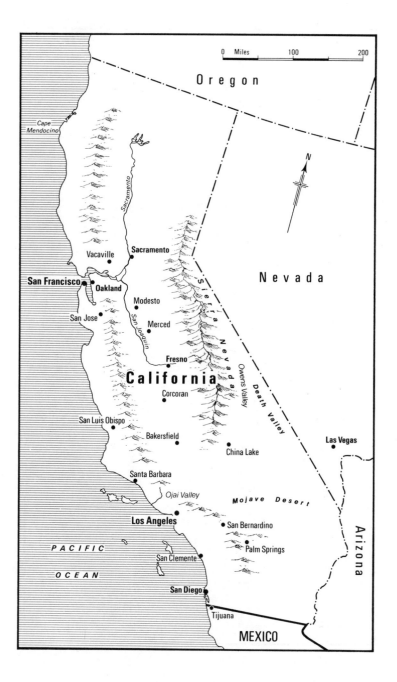

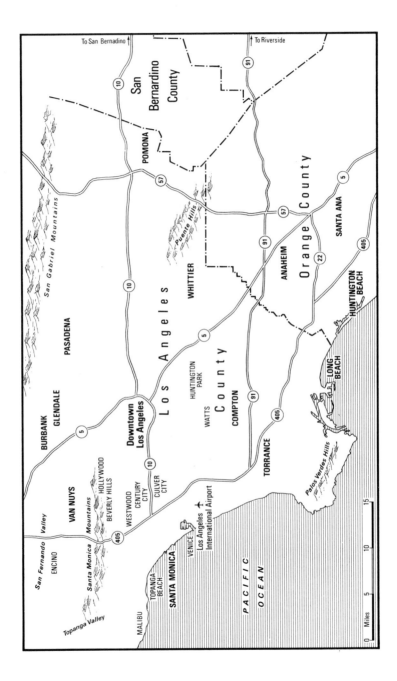

Contents

MEDIA MADE IN CALIFORNIA

1
California
Dreaming

"I'd be safe and warm if I was in L.A.—," wrote a sixties song-writer,[1] "California dreamin' on such a winter's day." Many of the dreams of American popular culture before and since the sixties come made in California; California themes provide a vital slice of the content of modern entertainment media. The industrial base of film, television, and popular music is now largely in California, their personnel belonging to what we will call the Beverly Hills occupational community. Because the state hosts this community—Hollywood—California lays claim to be called "state of the media."

But Hollywood is not all of California. True, its politics have been colored by Hollywood people, from Louis B. Mayer to Ronald Reagan. The Hollywood connection touches the state's economy: an estimated four-fifths of the recording industry's $4 billion-a-year product turns over locally. Undeniably, California society has been changed by the proximity of stars — of big screen, little screen, disc, and governor's mansion.

1. John Phillips of the Mamas and the Papas.

Despite all that, California's very size, history, and geography would have made its media fairly special. Our case is that California's media—its newspapers and broadcasting—show heightened typicality. For example: California's press dynasties are not unique. The long-run decline of family ownership of newspapers is demonstrated in other states. Yet California's dynasties seem to illustrate the phenomenon with a sharp clarity. The state offers for study the infertile Copleys of San Diego, the disputatious Knowlands of Oakland, the canny Chandlers of Los Angeles, and the filial Hearsts of San Francisco.

One of the most acute observers of California once referred to the state as the "great exception."[2] Yes, the growth on the West Coast of the entertainment divisions of the mass communications industry has made exceptional the state's participation in American media. But our case does not just rely on claims for Hollywood's or California's uniqueness. The organization of the Beverly Hills media community must be seen through lenses that take in New York as well as Los Angeles. The multiple differences of East Coast and West Coast (for example, between high culture—news programing—and low culture—entertainment) run through the book. One illustration: the Screen Actors' Guild, though present in New York, has become a special California form of labor organization within the entertainment industry. Many of the Beverly Hills community's members are transplanted New Yorkers. The westward trajectory of their careers has marked their lives and their work, and the community they have joined.

The "Great Exception"

The peculiarity of California is itself a potent American cultural myth. As long ago as 1934, *Time* magazine was writing about California as "a phenomenon as well as a state . . . California blinks its eyes from the glare of klieg lights in hysterical Hollywood, is lulled by the mission bells of Santa Barbara. Anything can happen in fabulous California."[3] But the myth was built on fact. California's is a unique physical environment,

2. Carey McWilliams: *California: The Great Exception.*
3. *Time,* October 22, 1934, p. 13.

shut off from the rest of the United States by desert and mountain, the home of an encyclopedic range of flora, climates, and topography. This is a disaster territory; the suburban sprawls around the San Francisco Bay Area and Los Angeles are routinely shaken by earth tremors. Each autumn the hilly country around Beverly Hills is threatened by the hot desert wind known as the Santa Ana. It fans brush fires at astonishing speed toward the wooden structures of celebrity homes. Drought and deluge alternate. In 1975–76, Los Angeles received 7.22 inches of rain; two years on, it had 33.44 inches, over four times as much.

Visitors to the state often remark that California seems somehow artificial: the green grass, the exotic trees and brilliant lemons and oranges. Indeed, these are artificial in the sense that they depend on water piped vast distances from the north of the state. In no other state does so much wealth depend on the supply of water; the city of Our Lady of the Angels is, by nature, semi-arid. But years before the movie industry arrived with its new methods of advertising images, the southern Californians were skilled at selling the lush attractions of their state. The health properties of local oranges were sold in the East by the California Fruit Growers Exchange (established in 1905), which later adopted the brand name Sunkist. An entire mythology of the California missions was dreamed up; massive resort hotels, like the all-wood del Coronado on the sandbar opposite San Diego, were opened. The purpose was to sell real estate. Just as the Bay Area's economy took off on the promise of gold from the Sierra, so that of Los Angeles took flight on a boom made of land, oil, and the movies.

But to Carey McWilliams, California was exceptional for reasons unconnected with the location of the movie industry. McWilliams had firsthand experience of state politics. From gold rush days, Californian political parties had been weak, while direct democracy quickly grew into a strong tradition of popular government. Between people and politicians were a set of unusually strong newspapers. Editors and journalists from both San Francisco and Los Angeles had a major part in the political reforms of 1911 which deliberately cut back the powers of political parties, substituting for them a set of electoral devices (including California's famous propositions) which left people distinctly dependent on the media for political information and leadership.

In California, in the 1930s, modern multimedia—the press, radio, film, the apparatus of "public relations"—were for the first time used in mass political campaigning. The husband-and-wife team of Clem Whitaker and Leone Baxter pioneered methods of media-based vote-getting later adopted elsewhere in the United States. California was their proving ground; they urged one of their candidates for governor to smile more for the cameras, and they created a proprietary image of his happy family. Thus they helped elect Governor Earl Warren, later Chief Justice of the United States. Among their successors, the campaign management firm of Butcher-Forde undertook the selling of the tax-cutting Proposition 13 in 1978.

In 1934 a milestone was reached when Louis B. Mayer, head of MGM studios, deliberately had movie footage passed off as actuality to be used in the Republican gubernatorial campaign. The object: to defeat the Democratic contender, author Upton Sinclair, and his imaginative plan to End Poverty in California (EPIC)—one of a long line of utopias made in California, beginning with Henry George, and not exhausted by Ed Clark's California-based bid for the Presidency on the Libertarian ticket in 1980.

In California the passage from acting into politics has been smooth. The skein of celebrity is unbroken: politicians become stars and vice versa. One day in 1967 while walking through the lobby of the Beverly Hills Hotel, several women thought they recognized a Californian politician who, following his defeat for the governorship, had returned to private law practice. "Say," one of the women is supposed to have inquired, "aren't you a motion picture actor?" The confusion was forgivable. The defeated candidate was Jerry Brown's father, Edmund G. Brown, Sr.; he had just been replaced in Sacramento by motion picture and television actor Ronald Reagan. Reagan had followed a hallowed trail into California politics. One precursor, Congresswoman and ex-actress Helen Gahagan Douglas, had been defeated by Richard Nixon in a race for the United States Senate in 1950. Reagan's mentor was George Murphy, U.S.

Senator from California, 1964–70, motion picture actor, dancer, and once Shirley Temple's leading man.

California as Source and Resource

Into the consciousness of the modern consumer of mass media have poured countless items of knowledge of California. Our psychic geography easily locates Sunset Strip. A generation of adolescents shed tears on Rosencranz Boulevard and followed the Beach Boys' little deuce coupe down to the Pacific Ocean. Haight-Ashbury is where, vicariously, the same generation reached adulthood. Downtown Burbank is ridiculed wherever Rowan and Martin's comedy series is sold. Cinemagoers and television watchers have ridden the intersections of Grant and Market, of the Santa Monica and Harbor freeways, countless times.

Media California is often with us. Early evening the glamor cops of *CHiPs* celebrate the romance of the California road; the aura is still there as private eye Cannon slides himself behind the wheel on the late-night re-runs. The beach life, brightly lit, car-bounded, media-saturated existence has become part of a highly valued style of living, available at the end of the westward trek. Stars head west, or are made in the West: we understand stardom nowadays in large measure as it comes from the physical circumstances of California living. The movie colony of early Hollywood laid the groundwork. Led by Douglas Fairbanks and Mary Pickford, magnificent pioneers, modern celebrity was universalized from a California base. Stars had pools, patios, and privacy—but privacy in the midst of intense publicity engineered by a new breed of West Coast professional publicists. Stars, by definition, ate at Chasen's and the Brown Derby and had beach houses at Malibu. Later, being a star meant being accessible for self-aggrandizing conversations with Merv Griffin or Johnny Carson; or, for a lower order of star, beaming from behind a giant square on *Hollywood Squares*. Stars have long bought or rented tracts of real estate in Holmby Hills, Bel Air, or Beverly Hills, whether their stardom emanated from music, films or, like Richard Nixon and Pat Brown, from politics.

Through the media California has provided styles of living—from health faddism to wine drinking and astrology. And styles of dying. In the 1950s *Dragnet* introduced us to the heroic cop patrolling the dangerous streets of Los Angeles. It was a dark side of the California dream, its authenticity attested by the program's relentless insistence that it derived stories from local police records. On his heels followed an endless array of Colombos, Starskies, and Mannixes: the popular iconography of crime is now palm-fringed.

In California the real and the fictional have a habit of running together. The state is a source of real-life horror, lovingly chronicled by newsmen playing up the stereotype of the oddball state. Executives of the major news agencies UPI and AP assured us that their counterparts in New York edited news copy in such a way that the California horror stories got more play than those from elsewhere. When asked to name their top ten stories from the later 1970s, these same executives turned up a startling list. Named were the Zebra killings in San Francisco, a seemingly endless series of savage murders by black killers that made *The Streets of San Francisco* as patrolled by Karl Malden seem uneventful by comparison. The list also included the mass murder/suicide of the People's Temple—one in another long line of fringe religions settled in the far West; and the tale of Patty Hearst. The Hearst affair, dramatic enough in real life with its shoot-outs and burn-outs on prime-time television, passed almost immediately into dramatic fiction. The tele-film version screened on ABC in 1979. Meanwhile the FBI agent who finally broke the case has the honor of being impersonated on screen by former *Gunsmoke* star Dennis Weaver, then himself evolves into celebrity in his own right. He writes the book of the story, becomes a television consultant, and ends as media man appearing as a crime reporter on television station KPIX in San Francisco. The speed of such evolution is uniquely Californian.

The One and Only Hollywood

We take Hollywood to mean not merely the tawdry Los Angeles city district of that name, but the occupational community that spreads across much of northwest Los Angeles County and is centered approximately on the municipality of Beverly Hills. It has certainly spread far beyond the Hollywood of the silent movies, which were followed west by sound motion pictures, then by network radio; then network prime-time television and game shows. The talk shows came west later, along with television's "long forms"—made-for-TV movies, mini-series, docudramas. Finally, popular music recording settled in the West. Each wave has contained an element of "one step east for every two steps west": New York retains a stake in all media forms. As the power of the three great television networks is reduced by the growth of the new forms of domestic video, we predict that the balance of media power will tilt even further west, since much of the programing of the new media will surely come from Hollywood. But New York may also see a contingent revival of television production.

"California" is as much an organizing principle in the modern media as a geographical description. For example, California is the place where both performers and forms cross over, spin off, and conjoin. Among the specifically "California" media jobs are those uniting different skills, conjoiners or hyphenates. Production success in motion pictures increasingly belongs to the writer-director: for example, the California film school graduates, George Lucas and Francis Coppola. A rising figure on the production horizon is the agent-producer, whose role combines representation of a single client in the old theatrical tradition with the movie producer's job of uniting the elements of a film or television production. Sue Mengers, an agent who by the late 1970s was one of the most successful in Hollywood, put together the writer, director, and stars for *A Star Is Born* (1976). Mengers herself represented several of these elements. The final product was a musical version of an original screenplay about life in Hollywood that first saw daylight in the 1930s and had twice since been made into films before Mengers's client, Barbra Streisand, got her teeth into it.

Another feature of the community is the spin off. Legitimate and bastard, spin offs make the Hollywood schedules roll. Only in California can a hit movie beget a television series; a hit record—*Ode to Billy Joe*—begat a movie. *The Mary Tyler Moore Show* begat *Rhoda* begat *Lou Grant*, an everyday tale of the life of Los Angeles journalists working for a paper with a distinct resemblance to the *Los Angeles Times.*

Such Texan products as *Urban Cowboy* (1980) and *Dallas* are unmistakable Californian products even if partly filmed on location. *Urban Cowboy* was the product of two years of haggling and negotiation in the Beverly Hills badlands between popular music and movies. *Dallas,* put together by Lorimar in MGM's Culver City studio, deliberately echoes an earlier Hollywood success—the movie *Giant* (1956).

But California is par excellence the place where crossovers occur. Television series star Robin Williams (who was discovered at the local Sunset Boulevard Comedy Store) crosses over into records and movies; singer Kris Kristofferson becomes an actor, and actor David Soul (of *Starsky & Hutch*) becomes a singer. Crossing over also occurs between the media and politics, between sport and the media, and so on. The William Morris agency in Los Angeles has among its clients not only a sizable slice of all the major entertainment stars but also sports people and politicians such as Howard Jarvis (co-author of Proposition 13) and ex-President Gerald Ford. Ford resides at Palm Springs, Los Angeles's desert retreat and a favorite spot not only for ex-Presidents but also for ex-stars waiting for their agents to call and lead them into new and greener pastures.

Johnny Carson's *Tonight* show, recorded since 1972 in Burbank, is the lodestone of the Beverly Hills world of celebrity. On the show the institutional divides disappear completely. One April 1979 show gives an example. Carson had Sammy Davis, Jr., as his principal guest. Sammy confided that he was making a new record. Going to be a good one, asked Johnny? Certainly, said Sammy: the lieutenant-governor of the state of California is flying down from the state capital in Sacramento to oversee the production session. The number two man in California state politics—elected in November 1978—was Mike Curb, boy genius of the record industry in Los Angeles, the man who produced Sammy's great hit, *Candy Man.*

The One and Only California?

California's culture is super-absorbent, syncretic. It is, after all, a state of immigrants with, at least since 1945, a predominantly youthful and highly educated population. Thus, many have said, it ought to be a model for the entire United States. Analogies have been made with the state's flora: nearly every plant that grows anywhere in the continental United States can be found in California. So whatever happens, in a cultural sense, anywhere in the United States will show up in California.

Following this train of thought, some authors have concluded that the California media are characteristically synthesizing. California popular music, for example, has always been an amalgam of styles—from folk, country music, and Broadway. The West Coast sound was never, musically speaking, original in the compositions of, say, Jan and Dean. Their words and music together crystalized the leisure longings of youth across the United States. Disneyland, at Anaheim to the south of Los Angeles, performs a similar function. There the consumer can choose any conceivable world to enjoy—or at least those worlds conceived in Walt Disney's folk wisdom and his marketing men's calculations.

But against this way of thinking about California, there is the opposing idea, expressed in Ben Stein's *The View from Sunset Boulevard*. If the California media are like a gigantic Xerox machine for the rest of the United States, then in Stein's view the picture of America reproduced is warped and flawed. This way of thinking about California as un-American has a long history. The silent movie pioneers were reviled for corrupting the nation's morals; the scriptwriters of the sound era were attacked as Jews and crypto-Communists and accused of using the movies for political purposes.

We will examine these traditions later, for we want to have it two ways and regard California media as in part unique, but also typical of the rest of the United States and, again in part, in the vanguard of developments elsewhere. Chapters Two, Three, and Four explore California's uniqueness as presented in the content of the state's media and in the organization and culture of the Beverly Hills occupational community, a society with no counterpart anywhere in the world. But then we argue California's typicality: Chapters Five, Six, and Seven emphasize the clear picture California presents of trends and tendencies in American media at large: the concentration of ownership in the metropolitan press; the burgeoning of radio as a result of

FM radio's new selling powers and the federal deregulation movement; the invisibility in the media of ethnic minorities. The story of California's Hispanic population has resonances for almost every other state. Chapters Eight and Nine suggest that California, at once unique and typical, may be leading the way. For example: the selling of political candidates for local and state office by means of professional campaign consultancies; the emergence of the state politician as celebrity—and as recipient of campaign money from the media industries. Of this mixture of the typical and the exceptional are Californian dreams made.

2
California
on My Mind

The imaginative traveler through the state of California is constantly reminded of somewhere else, of places real and fictional, their names half-forgotten as movie and television titles, as the catch phrases of popular song, slip and slide in the space of memory. California looks like everywhere for a simple reason. The state's landscapes have doubled for all regions of the world. Like an infinitely versatile extra, California's topography has had a walk-on role in countless productions. The Ojai Valley played Shangri-La in the movie *Lost Horizon;* the Mojave Desert has been the Sahara; Camp Pendleton, on the coast between Los Angeles and San Diego, was once Iwo Jima; the Santa Monica Mountains, Korea. China Lake, its expanse fittingly lunar, was once the moon. California's landscape is a universal backdrop against which any story can play. Horror: the wet coast north of Cape Mendocino served for the movie *The Fog* (1980). Existential perplexity: a decade earlier, Italian filmmaker Michelangelo Antonioni used the starkness of Death Valley for *Zabriskie Point* (1969). And Californiana litters modern popular music. The state's place names run together like the answers on *Name That Tune.* Swallows—San Juan Capistrano;

Woody Guthrie—Los Gatos; remorse—Sepulveda Boulevard; little cable cars—Tony Bennett; canyons—Joni Mitchell . . . the list is long, and confirms California's hold on the mass imagination.

The Big Backlot

Within the studios at Culver City and Burbank, the purpose-built sets reproduce city streets, railroads, western towns, and New England villages. MCA-Universal aids its cash flow considerably with revenues from its tour round the studio backlot: one of the most solidly organized and true-to-life pieces of faking devised by man. The backlot does not stop at studio boundary fences. In 1974, Los Angeles City Hall issued just over 2000 permits to shoot film and television on public streets. The number has grown since. *Variety* reported in December 1979 that during that year some 6000 permits had been issued to film and television companies for location shooting in the city's streets. The cities of San Diego and San Francisco are favored close-by locations. When the streets of San Francisco were full of camera crews shooting crime stories in the early 1970s, the board of supervisors complained that the city's reputation was being sullied. It was a dubious proposition since no policeman as active as Steve McQueen (*Bullitt,* 1968) was to be found on the city's payroll. A policeman named Dan White was; and he later murdered the city's mayor.

California's appearance on screen has varied as the costs of home-town production and location footage have changed, and as the response of audiences to California's specialty, the outdoors action-adventure, has changed. Four eras can be distinguished. The first is early films. The Keystone Cops presented the original video image of the Los Angeles Police Department, a law and order organization that would never again leave center stage. The Cops performed against a background of dusty streets, raw suburbs, and recently planted palms. The Hollywood Hills were a representation of the Wild West for untold cowboy pictures. The whole city was a prop for the silent comics; artificial snow once blocked Hollywood Boulevard; downtown Los Angeles provided that celebrated tall building from which Harold Lloyd dangled in fake shot. As film-makers invested in sets and film production became organized the landscape retreated. Douglas Fairbanks scaled the walls of Baghdad in the United Artists backlot—their "real" location was immaterial. At this stage in the history of film, the bounds of the fictive world are nonexistent. Early reliance on outdoors was declining fast in the 1920s as the studios began instead to rely on their own backlots and specially built sets. With the talkie era, the trend intensified; Hollywood's early sound equipment stayed largely in the studio to focus on musicals and filmed plays.

This second era ends, roughly speaking, with the film *Singing in the Rain* (1952). This is a classic "California" film. Set in Hollywood, it is a film about early Hollywood but it mirrored the real California solely in its dependence upon piped water. It was entirely studio-shot. Outdoors did not obtrude, and the streets of Beverly Hills in the movie came straight from the backlot supply dump.

After the early fifties, as the crisis in movie production caused by television and the breakup of the theater-owning cartel is resolved, California starts to appear on television. Game shows and talk shows at first come predominantly from New York, but California has a stake in the situation comedies and early adventure series. The very first examples of these have California subjects. Although always manufactured in Hollywood, the long-running comedy series, *I Love Lucy*, starring Lucille Ball and Desi Arnaz, took three years to "go California." The symbolical moment came when the fictional Lucy Ricardo packs up and leaves the couple's New York apartment, together with husband and the couple's loyal neighbors, Fred and Ethel. A bridge is crossed literally and figuratively as, in the episode aired on January 10, 1955, the four fictional characters drive across the George Washington Bridge en route to California. Lucy does not actually leave New York for good at that point; not for some years, and then to San Francisco. But after 1955 the plots are more varied, and more Californian. Instead of New York's snow and Broadway musicals (remember that fictional Ricky Ricardo played by Desi Arnaz is a band leader), the jokes and references switch to sunshine, automobiles, sports, and beaches—and to the Hollywood stars who crop up regularly in guest appearances. The life of Lucy, courtesy of Desilu Productions, acquires a California tinge. From around 1955 to about 1970, American television's distinct California slant is not matched in films: this was the era of "runaway productions" with a significant number of films financed by dollars but made in Italy, Great Britain, or Spain.

But in the later 1960s, films came back to Hollywood. Location shooting on Hollywood's doorstep once again enjoyed a cost advantage, and California themes and views seem since to have been more frequent. The techniques of modern television production favor outdoors action, and audiences like action-adventure series: California with its roads and hills and its supply of movie-trained professional stuntmen was the obvious place to make such programing. Thus by the early 1970s, the great bulk of prime-time television was not only produced in Los Angeles but much of it was filmed on the city's streets or, as we noted earlier, a short plane ride away in San Diego (the initial episodes of *Harry-O,* for example) or San Francisco. Much of the programing for formats other than "action-adventure" was, by 1970, also made in Hollywood. The squeals and laughter of the game shows belonged to California audiences. Proximity to celebrities was always important. One by one the talk show hosts abandoned New York for the West Coast; there, Merv Griffin's biographer[1] explains, the talk show host could find better guests and could himself embellish his career by appearances elsewhere in Hollywood or in Las Vegas. Situation comedies are mostly recorded in front of live audiences in Los Angeles. Their settings, however, are less frequently California than those of the series. Minneapolis, Philadelphia, and of course New York, are more often their fictional locations. In theatrical films, California is less dominant but is still easily the most common location. Of eighty-six theatrical films under production between April 1979 and April 1980, about 38 percent were being filmed in Los Angeles; some 47 percent were being shot somewhere in California. Second in choice as a location was New York with 17 percent. London, England,

---

1. Michael B. Druxman: *Merv,* New York, 1976.

was third. Far behind, a sizable spread of locations—Canada, Mexico, France, Florida, Arizona, Chicago, New Jersey, Texas, Kansas, and Massachusetts—contested fourth place. Within the United States, California and New York/New Jersey were completely dominant with about two-thirds of filming.* We reached a similar conclusion when examining film plots and fictional locations, though we admit that trying to quantify the importance of California is difficult. We looked at *Variety*'s reports of new feature films released during the years 1950, 1960, 1970, and 1980. The data are too sketchy to permit much generalization. Suffice it to say: explicitly California locales and themes appear with a frequency greater than randomness would indicate. A significant fraction of the "California" movies are crime pictures. New York is a locale and provider of film plots in roughly the same proportion as California. Films with an ethnic content appear to be usually California and New York based. There is a limited number of specifically California sub-themes: beaches, "life style," driving, and youth pictures are among them. A substantial number has an unspecified setting and a "nongeographical plot"—but cannot completely conceal the fact that they were filmed in California. The disaster and airport formulas are often Californian in this sense.

The proportion of California content in feature films appears to have grown over the decade of the 1960s. By 1970 more than a third of the movies with locales identified by name in *Variety*'s reports were "Californian." In the latter six months of 1970 seventeen identifiable titles were Californian. These included the memorable—Sidney Poitier playing a black detective in San Francisco in *They Call Me Mr. Tibbs*—and the ephemeral—*The Beverly Hills Call Boys*, shot on location in a Los Angeles brothel and said by *Variety* to be 100 percent homosexual pornography. Of the movies released, and reported in the period from March 26 through May 21, 1980, four had identifiable California components. One was based on the celebrated Los Angeles murderer nicknamed the Hillside Strangler (*Hollywood Strangler*). Another satirized the California life-style of the inhabitants of Marin County (*Serial*).

*Based on *Daily Variety*'s film production chart April 27, 1979, September 28, 1979, and April 4, 1980. These proportions are approximate.

Such numerical measures are rough and ready, and are perhaps better expressed in this way. California content varies according to the media form: in descending order of such content, the forms are: (1) action-adventure series for television; (2) game shows and talk shows; (3) made-for-television movies; (4) theatrical feature films; (5) television situation comedies; (6) popular musical recordings.

California Media Imagery

California imagery begins, appropriately, on the trek westward. Enough threads of American popular culture are stretched out between New York and Los Angeles, between East Coast and West, to weave a fine garment. One theme is the hijacking or chase along the great west-bound highways—Interstates 10 and 40.

California was where Al Jolson was coming. Otis Redding left his home in Georgia for 'Frisco Bay. Frank Sinatra and any number of middle of the road crooners have at one time or another left their hearts in San Francisco. San Francisco beckoned the young men who became the "beat poets" of the late 1940s and 1950s; Jack Kerouac's novel *On the Road* is a celebration of movement west. The theme reappeared in sub-literary form in the television series *Route 66,* in which the picaresque adventures of its heroes, two young men in a Corvette, suited the series form well. Route 66 once led west into southern California. Along it in real life traveled Janis Joplin from Port Arthur, Texas (to find freedom first in the then Los Angeles hippie community of Venice, later in Haight-Ashbury). On the same route had previously come the Joads in John Steinbeck's novel *The Grapes of Wrath.* The migratory farming family was put on the screen by Darryl Zanuck when the novel was turned into a film—though not before Zanuck had sent a private detective to check that the conditions in Californian farming were accurately described by Steinbeck. In the film, Tom Joad is played by Henry Fonda. His children, Peter and Jane, found California as paradisal as the Joads were promised. Peter took the same road, in reverse. His film *Easy Rider* (1969) was a description of the journey from California to a menacing eastern state where motorcycles were suspect and drug consumption persecuted.

California's history is bound up with travel: people came first to find gold, then to acquire land for farming. The imagery of traveling in order to find something valuable has lasted into twentieth-century media production. Sometimes the goal is unspecified, as when the heroine of southern California novelist Joan Didion takes to the Los Angeles freeways in the book-turned-film *Play It As It Lays* simply to find herself and to take part in the ebb and flow of traffic as a kind of reassurance. Drive-time, car travel, is what the economic and social infrastructure of California's two main urban areas depends on, so perhaps the themes of California fiction and music inevitably reflect motion.

The state's indigenous folk demons, the Hell's Angels, were distinctive by their mobility. Gangs clad in leather and riding powerful motorbikes first appeared in media consciousness when the group swept down on the town of Hollister in northern California in 1947. These cyclists appeared in fictional Hollywood form, with Marlon Brando terrorizing the popular imagination in *The Wild One* (1954); Roger Corman later had Peter Fonda and Nancy Sinatra don their leathers in *The Wild Angels* (1966). California newspapers, especially the *San Francisco Chronicle* and *Examiner* in their sensationalist heydays, took reams of copy from their doings—often, as Hunter Thompson showed in his book *Hell's Angels, "A Strange and Terrible Saga,"* as legendary as those of the Greek gods. For their alleged debauchery on the sands outside Monterey in 1965, the leader of one band of Angels—founded in 1950 in the town of San Bernardino where the Los Angeles metropolis meets the desert— reaped the ultimate Californian reward of film, television and talk show offers. Thompson did not think the threat real, more a question of Associated Press, *Time,* and *Newsweek* playing the California card with stories on the latest West Coast styles. But the Angels' aura was still strong enough in 1979 for *Rolling Stone* magazine to give them its cover and several inside pages, and real enough that when we went to interview *Rolling Stone's* West Coast editor in San Francisco a handwritten notice was attached to the office door saying that it had moved to New York. This was to mislead avenging Angels who had threatened to wreak violence on *Rolling Stone* for its exposé.

Motion was at the heart of the Californian youth culture of the 1950s and 1960s as relayed to the world by film and television: especially automobile idolatry. Cruising the streets was, still is, an established Californian pastime. The impact of a related activity—customized car and van production—on writer Tom Wolfe was so strong that he thereupon abandoned regular journalism for a more exotic form of writing. On returning from California he wrote *The Kandy-Kolored Tangerine Flake Streamline Baby* (1965). California's youth culture was demographically based on the postwar baby boom, even bigger in a state with a high proportion of immigrant families. Youth culture could be afforded, thanks to the state's economic expansion after World War II. When the rest of the United States caught up, California models were there to be copied. (Vance Stickell, head marketing man at the *Los Angeles Times,* told us that Detroit's car stylists keep a close eye on certain Los Angeles custom car shops.)

From cruising Van Nuys Boulevard in a customized car, it was only a short hop to the Pacific Ocean. The ocean meant surfing and beach life. It did not matter if there were few ten-foot waves in Denver or that no one in their right mind would try to surf off the Jersey shore, the glorification of southern California beach life was universally available. The career of the California quartet, the Beach Boys, is instructive here. Their early music was as much a celebration of hot rodding as it was of surfing. But cruising the roads and cruising the beach were kindred activities. "I've a tank full of gas and I'm really gonna move," they sang, "down to the beach where the surfers all groove." The litany of pleasure rang out: sun, fun, sand, surf, and girls, California girls. The trek west was worthwhile.

Hollywood has never since stopped making beach pictures, with titles like *Wild Bikini,* as part of its production for the drive-in trade. *Variety,* in April 1980, carried advertisements for a film called *Malibu High,* said likely to do well, albeit briefly, during the summer holiday season. But it was the popular mu-

sic industry that seized the possibilities of age-specific product with a California tinge and marketed it around the world.

If California music has any particular aural characteristic, it is the fact that it is recorded music, engineered and produced to the highest "state of the art" standards. Perhaps because of the traditions of the film studios, the expansion of Los Angeles as a center for popular music in the 1960s was marked by high quality studio work, including back-up musicianship. A nucleus of session musicians formed behind many of the Los Angeles hits of the 1960s: it included musicians later to branch off on careers of their own, such as Glen Campbell, Leon Russell, and David Gates.

Thematically, there is no single West Coast sound—even if the recording industry planned that the same consumers who had ridden in the Beach Boys' hot rod might also harken to Scott Mackenzie's beckoning toward San Francisco during the summer of 1967 (and wear some flowers in their hair). Three periods when California has been in the vanguard of popular musical developments were in Los Angeles between 1964 and 1968; in San Francisco from 1965 to 1969; and in Los Angeles again in the 1970s. The first was the time of such groups as the Byrds, Sonny and Cher, the Turtles, the Doors, Stephen Stills; rich harmonies, witty and not too inaccessible lyrics; the freedom to experiment with and assimilate musical trends that originated elsewhere (such as contemporary "protest" song). The second was when an interlocking set of San Francisco performers, an experimental radio station, and a local tradition of large-scale concerts jelled in a "scene" that was recognized internationally. Drugs, pseudo-revolutionary stirrings, and libido were celebrated by such groups as Jefferson Airplane, the Grateful Dead, and Country Joe and the Fish. The third period gave rise to what is now usually thought of as the West Coast sound and refers to the mellow "laid-back" style of the Eagles, Warren Zevon, and Jackson Browne. Musically, the West Coast is the proverbial melting pot where country and original rock could meet and marry (in Creedence Clearwater Revival) while middle-of-the-road pop could flourish close by (Neil Diamond, a darling of Hollywood proper); and weirdness bordering on

the genuinely original (Frank Zappa and the Mothers of Invention) was tolerated. The work of Zappa illustrates neatly what we earlier called the syncretism of Californian culture. Other artists have claimed that Zappa's work relies heavily on borrowing from other performers, notably from Captain Beefheart. Indeed, Zappa's work is amazingly eclectic. He discovers, on the streets of Hollywood, a half-mad man who sings discordantly to himself; Zappa records him in his own studio, releases a record and makes the man, Wild Man Fischer, an international but still discordant celebrity.

California has always been home to outsiders, real and fictive. San Francisco newspaperman Herb Caen claims to have coined the word "beatnik" to describe the denizens of the North Beach district of the city. There Neal Cassady, Allen Ginsburg, and a colony of friends and admirers were ensconced (in the same part of town, incidentally, which forty years previously had thrown up California's greatest capitalist, the founder of the Bank of America, A. P. Giannini). The eccentricities of the Beats gave a useful twist to the mythology of San Francisco and added useful circulation to local papers. A few years on these papers revealed to a waiting world the existence in San Francisco of the world's first ever topless bar. By then Herb Caen, who had worked for both the *Examiner* and the *Chronicle* in San Francisco, was well into a journalistic career which had consisted of mythologizing, in the most elegant of ways, the city of San Francisco. The identification and glamorization of "hippies" in the 1960s followed naturally on.

San Francisco has been weaving salable myths around itself since its birth in the Gold Rush. To successive generations of film- and television-makers San Francisco has represented intrigue and historical thrills; the earthquake, white slavery, the "houses" along the Barbary Shore, Chinatown. It helped that locations were only a train ride or quick flight away from Hollywood: the city was all too close for comedian Fatty Arbuckle, pilloried by the Hearst press in 1921 for his alleged sexual misadventures in one of the city's hotels.

Writers have been mesmerized by California's chiaroscuro: its bright light and dark deeds. Both San Francisco and Los

Angeles have been the locales for so many episodes of criminal behavior—and its detection—that the popular imagination has come to impart to crime West Coast characteristics.

Jack Webb, the producer/director/star of *Dragnet* (1951–59, 1967–70) had three Los Angeles policemen on his production team digging up corpses, strangulations, and attempted suicides from the LAPD's files. Webb's spiritual successor was former Los Angeles policeman Joseph Wambaugh. While an officer he wrote best-selling novels about the job; he became a full-time screenwriter and later invested his literary earnings in movie projects of his own—like Webb, seeking full control and LAPD authenticity. Thus the movie *The Onion Field* (1979) was a notorious Los Angeles case involving the murder of an officer out on the highway to Bakersfield. Wambaugh's accolade came in 1980. The fall television schedule had a series based on a Los Angeles policeman who wrote best-selling novels about the job in his spare time.

Crime, California style, is bizarre. And here fact lends a hand. Barely a few years after they occurred, first the Manson, then the Patty Hearst cases reappeared on television as telemovies—their real-life gruesomeness toned down for the domestic viewer. West Coast crime is well lit. The sun spotlights the well-dressed police officers, with dark glasses, and suntans, and beautifully laundered shirts. In *Policewoman,* action occurs, appealingly, on a beach, or a dusty hillside overlooking the city. In *Starsky & Hutch,* the detectives' flamboyant red and white car flashes along palm-lined boulevards. For California crime is action-packed: the streets are wide, the freeways available for chase and arrest. San Francisco is best because of its inclines; but in Los Angeles there are off-ramps galore, and escape routes at every intersection.

West Coast crime is patrolled by, and reflected on, by a unique band of private detectives, too. Raymond Chandler's Philip Marlowe is the media ancestor of an intentionally more comic private eye in *The Rockford Files.* The landscape, the long drives, the spacey quality of Greater Los Angeles match a particular type of existential detective-hero, of which Chandler's Marlowe remains the paragon. The scale of the urban area is baffling; the façades of the grandiose mansions in the hills

front not elegance but crime and corruption; everyone is concealing something behind a glossy front; dubiously acquired wealth is ostentatiously flaunted . . . and the existential detective ponders it all. Rockford has his mobile home symbolically parked by the beach as a fixed folksy refuge from the relentless motion of the city; Robert Mitchum, or Elliott Gould, playing Marlowe in successive remakes of Chandler have spartan apartments, a counterpoint to the rococo splendor of their clients, victims, and traducers.

California on Celluloid—A Closer Look

California has often shown up on celluloid—and video-tape—in the form of Hollywood. At its broadest this may mean show-biz, the inhabitants, be they permanent or transitory, of the West Coast celebrity world. At its narrowest in *Sunset Boulevard* (1950)—that saga of would-be screenwriters and has-been stars—California appears as the pathology of a community eating its heart out. James Parish and Michael Pitts[2] have counted some three hundred titles in which Hollywood itself was the subject for movies produced between 1915 and 1975. Some writers have seen Hollywood's fascination with itself as an index of creative atrophy. For example, a common ploy in situation comedies is to introduce a guest show-biz star. Even adventure series on television are not immune. *CHiPs* managed during its 1978–79 season to work in a role for pop singer Lief Garrett as a pop singer needing the protection of the California Highway Patrol. Game shows are notoriously self-regarding: *Hollywood Squares* is probably worst. Non-Hollywood California obtrudes on such shows only in the shape of an audience whose sole function is to make applause and laugh, while occasionally sharing a local in-joke with the celebrities.

But California is sometimes able to look at itself on celluloid in a deeper way. Four 1970s' movies provide some evidence that the state's history, social structure, politics, even its demographics, are all potential screenplays. *Chinatown* (1974) succeeded within the lines of a detective plot in presenting Los

2. *Hollywood on Hollywood*, Metuchen, N.J.: Scarecrow Press, 1978.

Angeles water politics of the 1920s and 1930s—even to the extent of suggesting the name of one of the city's great water-gatherers (William Mulholland) through its fictional engineer Hollis Mulwray. As well as being a vehicle for stars Jack Nicholson and Faye Dunaway, the movie probes some of California's darker reaches. Nicholson is an existential detective beneath his flippant exterior. He confronts the city puzzled. And the film's very title has meaning only at the film's end with gunplay in Chinatown, an incident that will be papered over so that respectable people never hear about it. *American Graffiti* (1973) as well as being the film that made George Lucas, its director, was a paean to musical nostalgia. It said that the California youth of its director, captured on film by means of location shooting in the northern California town of San Rafael, was universal. It turned into a full-scale Hollywood celebrity Wolfman Jack, a disc jockey who had broadcast into California in the 1950s from a Mexican station: a figure known to the youth of the West became known to us all. The film's illusion was that life in Modesto, Lucas's home town in the California Central Valley, cruising the main street, was like life everywhere. It was not, but the illusion holds.

Shampoo (1975) is a film about Beverly Hills. To Pauline Kael in the *New Yorker,* "*Shampoo* expresses the emotional climate of the time and place. Los Angeles has become what it is because of the bright heat, which turns people into narcissists and sensuous provocateurs. . . . The movie gets at the kink and wilfulness of the Beverly Hills way of life (which magnetizes the whole world)." *The China Syndrome* (1979) combined action/melodrama with intense California concern about nuclear power. Its power station is near Ventana, a fictional amalgam of the Ventana wilderness near Big Sur and Ventura on the coast northwest of Los Angeles; a television station has the call letters KXLA that are just right for southern California; there is a freeway car chase, and so on.

Such plots fit the action-adventure format best of all. They involve outdoor Technicolor action, vehicles, speed, guns, stylized violence, and easily resolvable tension: *Starsky & Hutch* is an obvious example from the late 1970s programming; an extreme case was *240-Robert,* scenes from the lives of search-and-

rescue specialists employed by the Los Angeles County Sheriff's department. *CHiPs* features motorcyclists with the state highway patrol involved in various plots in and around Los Angeles; one week they take part in a motorcycle race (off duty) across the Mojave Desert; the next they are operating along the Santa Monica beach. Do they carry values with them in those motorcycle panniers?

A California World-View

Does the presentation of California in entertainment programing contain values, or even a view of the world? The sheer volume and heterogeneity of the output of the Beverly Hills media community rule out any simple answer. For nine years American television showed a comedy series called *The Beverly Hillbillies,* which revolved around a single joke: a naïve Ozark Mountains family transplanted to the wealth and sophistication of Beverly Hills. The joke was on Beverly Hills, for its city slickers and media sophisticates usually ended the episodes having been made to look ridiculous by the mountain people. Folk wisdom generally triumphed. If Beverly Hills can make itself the subject of plotting in this way, then whatever "messages" or values it projects can never be merely one-dimensional.

Yet some writers have argued that Beverly Hills values follow a single track. Ben Stein[3] has detected an anti-business ideology, apparent especially in situation comedies made in California. Programs show rich people as criminals and businessmen as conspirators against the public good. Thus, says Stein: "On television, the folk idea has been changed, so that while it is good not to be poor, it is bad to be rich."

Stein's argument is a latter-day version of the conspiracy theories often held about Hollywood: that living in California's sun and affluence somehow breeds up anti-American humors. Many producers are Jewish, says Stein, and are ipso facto ideologues. But Stein's argument relies heavily on a small number of situation comedies, which do indeed show a grossly sentimental view of life as lived in New York or Philadelphia: some

3. Ben Stein, *The View from Sunset Boulevard,* p. 144.

of these come straight from the stable of Norman Lear, whose own liberal and populist leanings are openly admitted. Stein is less happy with such other examples of television programing as the action-adventure series: which are in fact much more California. It is precisely when he talks of such series that his argument falls apart. For he admits (*ibid.*, p. 145): "The good people on television are slick looking men and women, up-to-the-minute, lithe and thin, in flashy cars and flashy clothes." This is true of the action-adventure series, such as *Starsky & Hutch;* but what precisely is wrong with the values of slickness, modernity, fashionableness? Stein doesn't say.

Stein has obviously been influenced by New Right ideas about the subversion of American business culture. To a New Right writer such as Daniel Bell, the media bear much responsibility for this. They carry the values of a modern popular culture which undermines the ethic by which capitalistic accumulation is sustained. To Bell, the values of California are hedonistic: easily achievable happiness, costless pleasure and unearned celebrity. Such values, according to Bell[4] engender high expectations of reward without corresponding expectations of sacrifice and effort.

To Bell even the action adventure series would be suspect, since slickness, modernity, fashionableness are part of the hedonistic package. But why should these values subvert American capitalism? Indeed, if California programing has any message, it is about consumption—upon which the successful functioning of the economic system depends. The maintenance of consumer demand is vital in the modern economy, and Bell ignores this. Hedonism in Bell's sense may be bad for production, but it is a vital lubricant of consumer purchasers, especially for purchases of leisure.

Looked at closely, much of Beverly Hills output intimates that a good life can be bought, and it puts emphasis on leisure living (based on a great volume of consumption). For example the movie *American Gigolo* (1980), supposed by some critics to be a puritanical critique of Beverly Hills life, is really a paean to male fashionableness, to the new legitimacy of large-scale

---

4. Daniel Bell, *The Cultural Contradictions of Capitalism*, New York, 1976.

male spending on clothes. The film's star is thinly disguised as a clothes horse for designer creations. The stylishness of highway patrol officers Poncherello and Baker in *CHiPs* is an invitation to ride chicly off into the Pacific sunset on a large purring motorcycle. Instead of Daniel Bell's estimate of normlessness as the central Californian trait, such programs are charged with esteem for an outdoors, mobile, high-income life style, and their message is that it is available to be consumed by one and all.

3
Beverly Hills:
Occupational Community

"Here's Johnny," cries ever faithful Ed McMahon, and on cue that prince of modern American mass culture moves across the Burbank sound stage. Johnny Carson's audience, 14 million a night during 1980, takes silent part in a conversation about the world of celebrity, California style. Until 1972 that world was New York. Now it is inhabited by *Tonight Show* guests from the movies and television made locally, the likes of Johnny's former next-estate neighbor in Beverly Hills, Sonny Bono, singer and ex-husband of Cher. These media Californians reside in and around the city of Beverly Hills and, like Johnny or Merv or Mike or Dinah, travel to work in Burbank, Hollywood, or west Los Angeles. Malibu and Santa Monica are their beaches, KNX radio their source of news, LAX their international airport, Palm Springs their desert resort, the San Fernando Valley suburbs the butt of their jokes, and Las Vegas their place for a club date across the state line. Such names are flags on the cultural map that Johnny Carson's audience has by heart. His ellipsis—that this little world is America—is the mass entertainment industry's ellipsis. But his audience does not misunderstand, since they already have California on their minds.

Northwest Los Angeles County is where Carson's show is made—along with Chuck Barris's game shows, prime-time television from Spelling-Goldberg, syndicated radio from Drake-Chenault, records from Warner, cartoons from Disney, and feature films from Fox. It contains a specialized occupational community with its own social and cultural dynamics, its own markers of ascent and descent. Fred de Cordova, producer of Carson's show, told us this: "People buy big houses in Beverly Hills when they're successful and have to move out when they're not." The community is pyramid shaped, with the superstars such as Johnny Carson, apotheosis of personality, sitting on top. Like the best pyramids, it is built on the backs of obscure masses—bit-part actors, grips, and groupies. Yet, Stan Montero of CBS Records' West Coast operation told us, "It's a lot easier to starve out here." He meant that California's sunshine and its supply of part-time work made waiting for the break into celebrity easier to bear than in New York. New York, of course, and London, have their own mass communications occupational community. But the Beverly Hills community is unique. Likewise its history. The early film-makers founded the community. But why did they come?

Movie Making in the Sun

Movie production did not come to southern California simply for the sun. Florida gets more. Nor was southern California's terrain the deciding factor. San Francisco, where the infant movie industry showed signs of settling, has landscapes as varied in its hinterland. The main reason for choosing Los Angeles was its cheapness. Unlike New York, where the industry began, land and labor were cheap. Los Angeles was a non-union city with a ready supply of cheap craft labor and a reserve army of laborers, the Mexicans. Exotic locations could be easily reached, in the early days, by electric street car. While the movie director scouted locations in his Lagonda, the cast would follow (cheaply) in a streetcar—just like the one driven by Richard M. Nixon's father.

Why the movies stayed put is a different issue. By the 1930s labor was not so cheap; it was starting to unionize in forms not

markedly different from New York's. For the first twenty years
of sound filming, roughly 1930–50, much filming was done in-
doors, thus wasting both sunlight and terrain. But Los Angeles
had become an incomparably better place to live, especially for
actors. Apart from the prosaic economic reasons—economies
of scale and the build-up of specialized ancillary services in the
Los Angeles area—location in the West had a vital ingredient.
Living in Beverly Hills allowed year-round tennis and a private
backyard pool and the chance to buy into what promised to be
a long-lasting property boom. The unprecedented celebrity of
the first generation of stars, Douglas Fairbanks and Mary Pickford in particular, had given life in Beverly Hills something
special. The California style was defined by world audiences as
an essential in the package of attributes that made celebrity.

Pickfair—the Greening of Beverly Hills

Perhaps Hollywood, the pre-World War I farming village
turned movie center, was bound soon to lose its rural charm.
By 1920 it had the mixed character of a commercial industrial
locale as well as a residential community. Further inland, to the
east, was stuffy Pasadena, the favored suburb of the "old families" of Los Angeles. Closer to the ocean and to the foothills of
the Santa Monica Mountains was the obvious way to seek exclu-
sivity. Douglas Fairbanks and Mary Pickford led, and the pack
followed—before the stars drew up the drawbridge by managing in 1923 to defeat the efforts of the citizens of Los Angeles
to annex Beverly Hills.

In 1920, when Pickford and Fairbanks moved to their new
estate in the hills, the location was desolate. Soon, "Pickfair," as
the mock-Tudor mansion was named, looked out on eighteen
acres of green and a lake on which the couple canoed. Neighboring estates were occupied by Harold Lloyd, Ronald Colman,
David O. Selznick, and Charlie Chaplin: the greening of Beverly Hills was under way. Sixty years of avid planting and
watering have turned it into verdant hillsides of dense vegetation and obsessive privacy.

At leisure, Pickford and Fairbanks defined a style of celebrity life which has since changed little in its essentials. Fairbanks

popularized suntans; jogged; and propagandized on behalf of body massage. The couple established the vital principle of the transference of celebrity: that stars of one medium or dimension had lots in common with stars from another—all glittered equally in the California firmament. Since the traditional idea of celebrity in the 1920s hinged on aristocracy of birth, the crowned heads of Europe were welcome guests in Beverly Hills. The cinematic couple went to some lengths to embroider their own fairly commonplace backgrounds. Fairbanks, for example, hid the fact that his father was Jewish and persuaded star-struck journalists that he had attended Harvard. (He had not.) Subsequent denizens of Beverly Hills, and their professional publicists, proved highly creative in rewriting their personal histories. "Factoid" writing became a California form, and the facts in much writing about Hollywood were wonderfully embellished.

Why Television Production Went West

A passage as consequential as this was naturally the result of many factors: television economics; the crisis of the "major" film studios; stars' bargaining power; and innovation by individual directors and producers armed with a new conception of television entertainment programing.

Television in its early days in New York was financed and packaged by advertisers and produced by the advertising agencies. This inhibited creativity and stifled the special qualities of television; excessive attention to selling the goods detracted from audience enjoyment—as the higher ratings of the new less fettered Hollywood televison shows soon demonstrated.

The move west occurred because of a crisis in movie production: the studios were losing their audiences to television and, by court order of 1948, were also having to divest themselves of their lucrative chains of movie theaters. It was apparent that sooner or later they would have to accommodate the new medium. Warner Brothers was the first of the Hollywood majors to make a filmed series for television, for the 1955–56 season on ABC. Warners led a stampede, as first the technology then movie people became available for television.

A pull westward came from the large talent agencies, especially MCA and William Morris. Already based in both New York and Hollywood, such agencies saw an enormous opportunity for themselves if television production went west. In New York the "packaging" was done by advertising agencies; in Hollywood there was scope for the agents to put all the pieces together—actors, writers, and producers—and to get their 10 percent from each. MCA, led by Lew Wasserman, went further. It took over not only the packaging of shows but also production. By the 1960s, MCA-Universal was the top television production company.

The role of agents in the arrival of television in Hollywood was partly a reflection of the star system. The movies had created stars, actors, actresses, and mere personalities, and their newfound market power allowed them to choose their style of domestic life. And Los Angeles was the place to live, work, bring up children in the sunshine; it had more "creative space" than New York. Concern with ratings, by hooking shows to stars, drove television to Hollywood. Borrowing from the movies and from the Hollywood radio tradition of the 1930s and 1940s, television shows were deliberately constructed around starring roles. By the end of the 1950s it was not unusual for a television series star to be paid as much as the rest of the cast put together. For one 30-minute series-episode in 1959 star costs of $7500 versus other cast costs of $7500 were not unusual.[1] Stars of successful 39-episode television series were earning around $300,000 a year in 1959, excluding any additional earnings. This was little different from the million-dollar salaries of series stars around 1980.

Two series stand out as innovatory in their use of West Coast methods and elements. They made money—always a clincher. *I Love Lucy* we have mentioned before: it has a permanent place in television's ephemeral history. It first appeared on the CBS television network in October 1951. Lucille Ball was crossing over from a career as a modestly successful star comedienne in B movies and radio; Desi Arnaz was crossing over from his career as bandleader. Arnaz performed what to-

1. Irving Bernstein, *The Economics of Television Production and Distribution*, Los Angeles, 1960, pp. 70–73.

day would be called the function of "packager" and "executive producer," as well as being the co-star. Ball and Arnaz were keen not to have to move to New York—where nearly all television was being made. They had already spent much of their married life apart—owing to the war and Arnaz's band tours—and both were determined to stay in Los Angeles and bring up their young family there.[2]

The second show, *Dragnet,* originated in radio. Jack Webb, himself a crossover from films and radio, conceived a television version of *Dragnet* utilizing the space and mobility of Los Angeles (in contrast to the studio based crime shows made for television in New York). The West's "creative space" was important for both Webb and Arnaz because they were having to solve an interrelated set of new technical, financial, and creative problems. In the middle months of 1951 Arnaz developed the new television form of the situation comedy recorded on film with multiple cameras in front of an audience. The technical problems of filming and lighting were immense; there were other difficulties—for example, the legal and fire regulations that kept a big audience from entering a movie sound stage. These problems were more easily solved in the relatively relaxed conditions of Hollywood, away from the headquarters of the network and sponsor (CBS and Philip Morris).

Hollywood television by the end of the 1950s had set a pattern which has not altered materially since. *I Love Lucy* and *Dragnet* fixed the two dominant genres—the studio sitcom recorded before an audience, and the filmed action-adventure show. By 1960 the shows were being partly made by the large Hollywood companies and partly by independents led by "hyphenate" entrepreneurs such as Arnaz and Webb. This broad pattern remained set in 1980 (although the production companies had changed).

The Beverly Hills way of life was suited to television. Playing a major part in a television series, either in front of or behind the camera, was then and is now a gruelling business. For an actor on the series treadmill, one consolation is that some of the interminable series of meetings can be held, say, on the

2. Bart Andrews, *The Story of "I Love Lucy"*; Desi Arnaz, *A Book,* New York, 1976.

executive producer's breakfast patio; for the player in an action-adventure show, waiting between shots in December is pleasanter on the streets of the San Fernando Valley than in Brooklyn. For writers, too, California offered something special—to do with the syncretism of California's culture. Since all America is there in California, the writers seeking for themes, plots for their situation comedies, adventure series, found them easier to come by.

Record-Making in the Sun

In the 1960s and 1970s the attractions of Beverly Hills did not lessen. Scores of popular musical stars settled there because its mansions offered seclusion, privacy, and a nice place to recuperate. It offered the twin satisfactions of privacy from fans and proximity to publicity; also the traditional creature comforts of available restaurants and sexual encounters. Los Angeles, a major port close to Mexico, has always been a good place for buying drugs.

Commercial realities, as well as artists' preferences, explain why the American record industry is now predominantly headquartered in Los Angeles (an estimated 70 percent of record labels are based there). Los Angeles is the place for crossing over to new media forms and embellishing careers through the made-for-television film; the television musical; the music-based movie.

Thus some time between the conscription of Elvis Presley and the death of Janis Joplin popular music went west in two major senses. First, the movie industry grasped that age-specific youth music and performers could be linked to film: hence the string of Elvis Presley films and the relocation of Elvis as a cultural idol in the (traditional) confines of a movie star surrounded by the walls and vegetation of a Beverly Hills mansion, making occasional sorties to film studios and Vegas dates. Second, the West Coast was throwing up performers and market conditions which favored the suppliers of talent: after the A & R (artist and repertoire) men went scurrying to sign up new talent in San Francisco and Los Angeles, their corporate backers soon followed. Stan Cornyn, a Warner recording executive, told us that the attractiveness of the West Coast as a center for music production became overwhelming during the 1960s: "The West Coast had the resilience to embrace the new culture with its new modes of corporate activity; it was the environment chosen by the artists themselves." And chosen because the California life style had by then been incorporated as part of what being a star meant.

Since the golden days of Pickford and Fairbanks new media have arrived, but the quality of much of star life has remained the same. Actors' biographies and autobiographies, albeit notoriously unreliable accounts of their lives, provide evidence of the frenetic pace. Charlton Heston's *The Actor's Life*, which covers the years 1956–76 and is better than most of the genre, shows him dashing off to Europe more often than Pickford and Fairbanks ever could; but his running from tennis court to limousine to the VIP lounge at LAX differs only in color, not in shape, from the frenetic calendar of Pickford and Fairbanks. The model applies in television and popular music, too.

Neil Diamond, a pop singer moving toward the middle of the road, is displayed in *People* magazine as shuttling restlessly between Europe and the two American coasts on tours and visits. His home is in Holmby Hills; he does club dates in Las Vegas; during 1979–80 he had a regular commitment at Paramount Studios. He was acting, performing, and composing for the remake by Paramount of the original talkie, *The Jazz Singer*. Such is the life of the California crossover. In it Los Angeles often represents comfort, a place to relax.

The new rock music arrivals take their leisure coolly. The Eagles are a California group whose members live in the residential hills around Los Angeles. One of them, Ron Henley,[3] gazes down from his house above a canyon, and his view stretches as far as Catalina Island thirty miles away. "Wow," he says, "it still does it to me, when the sun's going down and those lights start to come on—I still get filled with wonder." As once did Pickford and Fairbanks.

---

3. Quoted in Anthony Fawcett, *California Rock California Sound*, p. 9.

Beverly Hills—Golden Ghetto

When we refer to "Beverly Hills," we are using the place name in two senses. The occupational community of the mass communications industry was never confined within the city limits of Beverly Hills; nonetheless there is a fairly strictly defined area in which the community's more affluent citizens choose to reside. These limits are, to the west the Pacific and the beach communities from Malibu south to Venice; to the north the Simi Valley; the Santa Monica freeway is a southern boundary.

Present-day Beverly Hills is a stuffy town. According to Walter Wagner, the chief citizens of the 5.7 sq. mile town are its realtors, its hairdressers, and its psychiatrists. Beverly Hills has long been an object of both admiration and envy. Charles Manson was one who combined these two attitudes. Manson seems to have been acting out his resentments against Hollywood, which he had tried to enter as a singer guitarist and which had rejected him. Manson and his group had at one point moved into the home of Dennis Wilson (of The Beach Boys) at 14400 Sunset Boulevard; Wilson was too frightened to remove them, and Manson's group did some $100,000 worth of damage. Wilson was obliging enough to take Manson Family members to his expensive Beverly Hills doctor to clear up their venereal diseases.

Manson and his "family" of mainly young female followers were no ordinary hippies. On consecutive nights in 1969 they attacked two casually selected houses in the expensive hills of northwest Los Angeles—brutally killing a total of seven people, including film star Sharon Tate and top Beverly Hills hair stylist Jay Sebring. The nine months' trial was equally sensational. Manson completely lacked remorse, and one of his women followers attempted in 1975 in Sacramento to assassinate President Ford.

The Manson story illustrates how Hollywood seems to attract outlandish people and behavior which enable the Los Angeles press—usually so adulatory of Hollywood—occasionally to run stories which present the factual melodramas of Hollywood as being stranger than Hollywood's own fictions. The Manson story presented by the other media also fitted well with eastern stereotypes of the "only in California" theme: decadent stars, dead bodies by the pool, messages daubed in blood on the walls, the hippie colony, the Los Angeles police (struggling to match the image of the professional scientific crime hunters of *Dragnet* but in practice appearing more like the Keystone Cops); and Manson himself—the video-genic villain, the unsuccessful Hollywood performer playing in a melodrama of his own murderous creation. It gave two local officials, assistant district attorney Vincent Bugliosi and coroner Thomas Noguchi access to TV cameras, and thus a boost to their political careers.

Star Career Trajectories

New York and Nashville are good places to start a star career; but the West Coast is where it "arrives." Gossip reporter Rona Barrett tells in her autobiography that a whole generation of future Hollywood stars were at one time (her youth) to be found in Downey's Restaurant in New York—Paul Newman, Peter Falk, and Sidney Poitier among them. Much may happen en route: black soul singer Ray Charles was, during 1979, endorsing a new brand of recording tape. "Sound systems," he emoted, "have come a long way since I left Jacksonville for Los Angeles": including the transformation of Ray Charles from a performer for an almost exclusively black audience into a major figure in the mainstream popular music market.

More stars now rise in the west. John Wayne, born Marion Morrison, was a local boy and University of Southern California alumnus; but it was for his star qualities that the Orange Country authorities renamed their airport for him after his death. Star-spotting is the classic Los Angeles activity. The story of the discovery of Lana Turner in Schwab's drugstore in Hollywood was a publicist's fabrication, but remains a potent myth. (Turner was a local high school senior whose physical charms had been under observation by studio scouts for some time before she was given an offer.) Los Angeles popular music and its comedy are nowadays two areas of entertainment where talent spotting has become institutionalized. One such institution is the Comedy Store.

Early in 1979, the Sunset Strip offered a strange sight: a motley collection of pickets proclaiming a strike under the banner "comedians for compensation." The sight was at once risible, and pathetic. This strike was at the Comedy Store, a showcase for comedians to demonstrate their talents in public. Until the strike, comedians worked for nothing: the inducement was the chance of being spotted by agents and producers. The chance is real because the demise of vaudeville and radio comedy deprived Hollywood of its recruiting mechanisms for comedians. In response to this show business need, two Comedy Stores came into being in Los Angeles, with others in La Jolla (San Diego) and San Francisco. Hollywood shows, including Johnny Carson's *Tonight* show, recruited young comics throughout the 1970s and in some cases gave them national fame. This is about the quickest upward career ladder in Hollywood.

Robin Williams went up the Comedy Store ladder, and became a television star with the series *Mork and Mindy* at the age of twenty-six. Raised near San Francisco, he attended the Juillard School in New York. After a brief stint at the San Francisco Comedy Store he moved to Sunset Strip's Comedy Store, where he was soon spotted. This led to television appearances on *Laugh In,* and one special appearance on *Happy Days,* the producer of which—Garry Marshall—then devised *Mork and Mindy.*

A different sort of Comedy Store career was that of Steve Lubetkin. A transplanted New Yorker, he performed in the Los Angeles Comedy Stores for several years for no pay. He appeared in an unreleased film. Lubetkin was active in the comedians for compensation strike; it seems to have added to his depression over his lack of career success. At the age of thirty he jumped to his death from a local hotel. He had never appeared on television; had a 16-year-old Buick and few clothes. His last paid performance was in Orange County at the Newport Beach "Last Stop Club," where he was paid $15.90 for a performance and emcee duties.[4]

At the same time Robin Williams—probably with more tal-

4. *Los Angeles Times,* Calendar section, July 15, 1979.

ent and certainly with better training—was negotiating to make his first theatrical film in the off season from *Mork and Mindy;* it was a remake with human actors of the cartoon *Popeye.*

Appearing in a local venue in Los Angeles is one way of entering the fiercely competitive record business. The city is dotted with clubs that have become showcases of talent both local and arrived from far afield. The most celebrated of such venues are the Troubadour and the Whisky; the former will live for a long time on its reputation as the place where Elton John was discovered. But talent recruitment in the popular music business is decentralized, so Los Angeles venues will never be as central a funnel for new talent as the Comedy Stores. Most record companies employ A & R staff to scour the country for new sounds.

The fast way west has always been on the basis of achievement elsewhere, usually New York. This was how the pioneers arrived, then the Famous Players, then the talkie stars. Certain agents, such as Leland Hayward, specialized in luring Broadway talent to Hollywood. Henry Fonda described Hayward's techniques (in Brooke Hayward's *Haywire*); the *New Faces* he mentions was a Broadway revue.

> He [Hayward] didn't show any interest in me until he saw me in *New Faces.* Then, when he did, . . . a wire . . . asking me to come to California. I wired him "No" I wasn't interested in films . . . He wired me back . . . one of those telegrams that went on page after page . . . I wired him back with the one word "No." Then he got me on the telephone . . . He said: "It won't cost you anything, I'll pay for your goddammed airplane fare and your hotel . . ."
>
> So I wound up flying out to California. He met me at the airport . . . He took me to a suite at the Beverly Wilshire hotel. I went in to shower. . . . when I came back out again, he was in the front room with Walter Wanger. I'd never heard of him before. He had no idea who I was either . . . We sat there, and within half an hour or so, I was shaking his hand on a deal. . . . for one thousand dollars a week. And it was my deal: I could go back to my beloved theatre in the winter . . . I just couldn't believe it.

The Family Life of Beverly Hills

One way into Hollywood is to grow up in it. Best of all, be a child of a Hollywood celebrity. Or have one of those stage mothers/personal agents who gets you started as a child actor; there are more than fifty agencies in Los Angeles which handle child actors, with television commercials the main work. If you want to enter one of the crafts, being in a Hollywood craft family will be an especially big help.

In a state often said to be the place where traditional kinship ties have dissolved—creating the market for the California support systems of exotic religion and est-type "personal dynamics"—family ties are impressively strong within the Beverly Hills occupational community. Here are some illustrations from the new California dynasties. Alan Ladd, Jr., was probably Hollywood's highest paid executive when he left Twentieth Century-Fox in 1979 to establish The Ladd Company. His father was Alan Ladd, the actor, who had married his own agent, Sue Carol. The son of the second marriage was David Ladd, who was married to Cheryl Ladd when she became one of *Charlie's Angels*. A daughter of the second marriage was Alana Ladd, married to Michael Jackson, dean of Los Angeles radio talk show hosts on KABC radio.

Take the Douglases. Michael, son of Kirk, co-starred in *The China Syndrome* (1979). Another of Kirk's sons, Peter, produced *The Final Countdown* (1980), in which his father starred. And Michael Douglas—besides starring in *The Streets of San Francisco*—was instrumental in bringing *One Flew Over the Cuckoo's Nest* (1975) to the screen. With talent, being the child of a star is an enormous advantage. One of the pleasures for actors of filming on location not too far out into the big backlot—say in Arizona—is that your children can visit you. Alan Ladd, Jr. (b. 1937), for example, observed almost the entire location shooting of *Shane* (1953), a useful experience for a teenager who already wanted to be a film producer.[5]

The family networks of Hollywood are extremely intricate. The first studio heads were notoriously good at looking after

5. Beverly Linet, *Ladd*, New York, 1980.

their own, and much of the "golden period" of Hollywood can be analyzed in terms of the alliances, dynastic marriages, feuds, and sibling partnerships of a few families of moguls. Take just the two top men at Loew's/MGM, for example—Nicholas Schenck and Louis B. Mayer. Nicholas Schenck's brother, Joseph, in 1935 became head of Twentieth Century-Fox. Louis B. Mayer's two sons-in-law were David O. Selznick (a top independent producer and himself the son of a founding-father mogul and the brother of a founding-father agent) and William Goetz—(the Goetzes were another great Hollywood family of this period). Through the golden period the big studios used family as a basis for recruitment; many young B movie producers hired in the 1930s were themselves sons of producers. Meanwhile the crafts were also at least as nepotist, as craft occupations usually are. One extreme example was the Westmore family—six brothers who between them achieved an extraordinary ascendancy in studio make-up departments.[6]

With the passage of years the family ties have grown more and more complex. New ones have certainly come into being with television. Take just Penny Marshall, the star of *Laverne and Shirley*, a show which was devised by her executive producer older brother, Garry Marshall. Penny Marshall married a man who had grown up down the street from her in the Bronx, Rob Reiner (of *All in the Family* fame), whose father was Carl Reiner, the prominent actor/writer/director.

The extent of family connections in Hollywood is enormous; it crosses media, marriages, and occupations. People may be linked by what is now an ex-marriage; or a TV cameraman may be the son of a movie actress. As in other occupational communities, Beverly Hills is cemented by a mixture of work and family connections.

The Local Campuses

Some mothers signify less than others, as is shown by the tortured relations over the years of the University of California, Los Angeles (UCLA) and the University of Southern California

6. Frank Westmore and Muriel Davidson, *The Westmores of Hollywood*.

(USC). These top local schools have been almae matres to generations of sons and daughters from the Beverly Hills occupational community. But despite the Californian affinity for higher education, Hollywood has remained remarkably impervious to recruiting its elite on the basis of professional attainment in mass communications as certificated by the universities. Again, it was Douglas Fairbanks who was instrumental in establishing the first ever course in film, at USC in 1929. But only in the 1970s did Hollywood begin taking graduates in film and television from USC seriously—ever since Francis Coppola proved that an intellectual, college-trained film-maker could also make lots of money, and that his college-trained buddies were hot too. Coppola did a graduate course in film at UCLA; his protégé George Lucas (*Star Wars*) emerged from the undergraduate program at the division of cinema and television in the school of performing arts at USC. Until then, Hollywood mass communications had no regular recruitment program. But southern California film education has now undoubtedly arrived. Names such as George Lucas, Randall Kleiser, and Gary Kurtz of USC, Francis Coppola and Paul Schrader of UCLA would inspire any local agent. It is not that many film school graduates penetrate the industry: few do. But Hollywood is now far more receptive, and at USC the staff is anxious not to upset that new special relationship.

"Production people rule the roost here," Dr. E. Russell McGregor of the USC cinema division told us. He did not mean it as criticism, for he extolled the practicality of the four-year undergraduate degree offered in his school. The present B.A. degree is an outgrowth of the first B.A. in film offered at the University in 1932. Admission is tough, and students are rigorously examined in film-making capacity. USC's official claim to be the top film school in the country holds up. But one point stood out from our discussions there.

It is the striking absence of Hollywood's fabled largesse. The film school inhabits buildings one grade above shacks; some equipment is cast-off at several removes. The largest recent endowment came from Ray Stark, a very recent addition to the roster of Hollywood moguls. The school's official spokesperson lamely says that "there is no tradition of philanthropy in Hollywood." But isn't the reason for Hollywood's meanness toward academic film education on its doorstep a deeper one: academics mean questioned assumptions, processes revealed, and publicity of a kind the PR men cannot control?

As if in response to this unspoken fear of Hollywood, the USC professors play down the critical side of their work—hence Dr. McGregor's remark. Students leave USC well equipped to make films, but underprepared in film criticism—and in the economics and structure of the industry they want so badly to enter. USC boasts among its teachers a journalist crossed over into academe, Art Murphy, formerly a staff journalist at *Variety*. Murphy specializes in the finance of film and television production and teaches the graduate course endowed by Ray Stark which prepares students for management within the industry. But Murphy is virtually alone. The regular student population is given little or no insight into the money processes, or Hollywood's peculiar trade-union structure.

A Variety of Daily News

The following is from an article in the *Los Angeles Times* (November 13, 1978). It illustrates that in the sun-kissed mass communication community of southern California, darkness has many uses:

> Several years ago, Hollywood publicist Stan Rosenfield had a client—a former actress—who was coming out of retirement to resume her career.
>
> Rather than simply announce her availability for film projects, Rosenfield decided to announce that she had already signed a contract for her comeback role.
>
> "The best way to get work in Hollywood is to make it look like you already have work," Rosenfield says. So he issued a press release that his client had been signed by British producer Roland Arch to star in *Mother of Pearls*, a movie about a nun who had escaped Nazi Germany with 12 orphans.
>
> There was, of course, no such producer and no such movie. But the *Hollywood Reporter* published a brief item. Three weeks later, Rosenfield sent out another release. Again the *Reporter* printed the item.

Emboldened by his success, Rosenfield released another story six weeks later; this time he promoted two of his clients—the "star" and another actress, who would "co-star" in *Mother of Pearls.* Sure enough the *Reporter* printed both the items and mentioned both clients.

But when questions, congratulations, and offers began to come in for the star client, she became embarrassed. To Rosenfield's surprise she asked him to get her out of it.

Dutifully Rosenfield put out another release and— voila—the *Reporter* announced that the actress "has requested and received her release" from the movie because of delays in filming.

"A few days later," Rosenfield recalled, "she was at a party, and an actor friend came up to her and said, "I hear you're not going to do the Roland Arch film after all. Good. I worked for him on a film last year and he's a real son of a bitch."

The story is not apocryphal. And it can be matched with, for example, the autobiographical details of his profession given by Henry Rogers, the impresario of Beverly Hills press relations.[7] He got Rita Hayworth her first major role by pure and simple lying, and he manipulated the Academy Awards in favor of Joan Crawford. In other words, fiction is a fact of Beverly Hills life. And the newspapers reproduce it.

Central to the occupational community is the Hollywood trade press. In addition to numerous weekly specialist papers, such as *Billboard* for the record industry, there are two daily "trades," *Daily Variety* and *Hollywood Reporter.* These papers appear on the desk of almost every executive; they are, proverbially, read first thing; telephone conversations that interrupt interviews are often about items in the day's "trades." Editorially, these two are about one-half factual reporting and businesslike reviews on industry events, products and trends, and one-half personality gossip inspired for the most part by press agents. Their advertising is plentiful, focusing heavily on announcements of movie and television projects.

Everyone in Beverly Hills says that the trades are indis-

7. Henry C. Rogers, *Walking the Tightrope: The Private Confessions of a Public Relations Man,* New York, 1980.

pensable—in a fragmented industry the only way of keeping up with the rush of events—yet at the same time all are cynical about the origins of many stories. Especially those in the *Hollywood Reporter:* "50 percent is true and 50 percent lies and the fun is finding out which." The daily trades are vital in two ways. The hundreds of showbiz reporters in Los Angeles are subscribers, so interesting stories in the trades tend to reappear, re-written, in the entire range of other media, both U.S. and foreign. The trades are also the main channel for talking to fellow members of the occupational community—look at me, I'm dancing, working, doing deals, etc. Much Hollywood hype is home-town hype.

The community knows that a fair amount of its embroidering of the facts will get into the trades and thus be re-used. It is partly because so much of the news is fabricated that the sober and much less gullible weekly edition of *Variety* is so valued. Corruption is subtle. For example, trade paper reporters are poorly paid, but they have access to top people in the industry; one result, it is claimed, is seduction by means of hints of job offers, of requests to read screenplays and the like.

Present-day corruption differs considerably from that which operated in the days of the big studios when two syndicated columnists dominated publicity: Louella Parsons (syndicated by Hearst) and Hedda Hopper (in the *Los Angeles Times,* New York *Daily News, Chicago Tribune,* and many others). They possessed highly concentrated symbolic power, and they pursued vendettas. They plugged their own favorites and were themselves used by the Hollywood majors to keep "difficult" stars in line. They used their positions to enrich themselves and their relatives; they both had highly lucrative radio (and later television) shows on which stars appeared and were rewarded with additional free publicity in the press columns.

Celebrity Hills

The modern newspaper columnist closest to Louella and Hedda in her power to confirm local celebrity is probably Jody Jacobs, society editor of the *Los Angeles Times.* The Jacobs beat is not show business, note, but Los Angeles society; the two run pretty close together at most times. Ten months' close reading of Jody Jacobs's daily tours of the new-rich, old-rich, arrivistes, and the justly famous produced the following observations.

Nearly all of the people who appear in the Jacobs columns have made their fortunes since 1930; much money has been made in the great Los Angeles boom since 1945. The old-wealthy families stand out, and chief among them the royal family of Los Angeles, the Chandlers, publishers of the *Los Angeles Times* and controllers of the Times-Mirror publishing empire. Jody Jacobs's sense of propriety means that the Chandlers appear only infrequently. However, readers are left in little doubt of the special links between, say, Mrs. Dorothy Chandler and the Los Angeles Philharmonic.

But Los Angeles society as defined in these columns revolves entirely around Beverly Hills; its origins reflect those of Hollywood. Many people, perhaps as many as half, are Jewish; blacks are few, and they include celebrities such as Sammy Davis, Jr. The starring roles in the columns are played, unsurprisingly, by stars. Mostly these are somewhat past the peak of their careers, even if, like Kirk Douglas and Gregory Peck, they are still active. The occasional appearance of Frank Sinatra at a local charity performance is big news, as is the sight of John Travolta in a restaurant surrounded by a football team of male companions. Younger stars appear less frequently—perhaps they are too busy becoming old stars. Rock music stars presumably still lack respectability.

The top flight inhabitants of the Beverly Hills community often spotted by Jacobs are the managers of the entertainment empires: Lew Wasserman of MCA, Dr. Julius Stein, Ray Stark. Here are the top publicists Henry Rogers and Warren Cowan, top lawyers, realtors, decorators, and hairdressers. Record executives, including Clive Davis of Arista Records and Neil Bogart of (until 1980) Casablanca Records & Filmworks, are included; passing politicians, Gerald Ford, Jerry Brown and ex-U.S. Senator from California John Tunney, too. Scientists, despite California's supply of distinction, engineers, and industrialists are missing. Since the Beverly Hills sport is tennis, the column records all the year-round pro-amateur tournaments featuring—yet more celebrities. Agents aplenty: one of the most sought of all invitations is to the party "super-agent" Irving (Swifty) Lazar throws on the evening of the Oscar awards. Few occasions are so larded with free publicity as the annual awards of the Academy of Motion Picture Arts and Sciences; few occasions display as clearly the rank orderings of this community, the anachronistic prestige enjoyed by the movies within it.

Oscar night is unusual in being a live show, broadcast on national television. On few other occasions are actors' acting abilities so tested. Home-town hype has its biggest outing on the Oscar circuit. The trade papers are enormously important. Several months before the great day full-page ads start to appear in *Daily Variety* and the *Hollywood Reporter.* The name of the game is to get the voters to see your film; to get them to the screenings or (more recently) to see the film when it is screened (free again) on the local cable system; to win awards from the numerous mini-Oscar contests, since, for example, the choice of the Directors Guild for best director is usually the choice of the full Academy.

Founded in 1927 with the active assistance of Louis B. Mayer and other studio chiefs, the Academy originally looked remarkably like a company union. Its first leaders were actors and its goals were mixed. Douglas Fairbanks, president in 1927, managed as we have seen to establish a course in film education. Meanwhile the Academy was instrumental in securing some concessions on hours and conditions for actors from the studio moguls. But after 1933, when the Screen Actors' Guild was established, the Academy became for some years an object of suspicion, a "tool of the bosses." Its membership declined from 800 to 400. By the later 1940s, however, it was reviving as an honorific, public relations body for the entire industry. Although the actors were still numerically dominant, the other areas of expertise got a share of the limelight. The Academy currently has some 3700 active members.

Actors	1200
Executives	200
Producers	260
Directors	200
Writers	345

Cinematographers	100
Art Directors	200
Film Editors	160
Music	220
Sound	190
Public Relations	180
Short Films	200
Members-at-large	250

Although the categories supposedly cover only films, many of those involved also work in television. The "Emmy" awards, presented since 1949 by the National Academy of *Television* Arts and Sciences (NATAS), have never been so prestigious, nor has the occasion been so Hollywood a one as the Oscars. In the 1970s Hollywood become increasingly resentful that it only had one-third of the NATAS board of trustees, the same as New York. In 1977 many television stars said in advance that they would refuse to appear, and NBC refused to televise a star-less Emmy Awards ceremony. A new body, now lacking the word *national* (and in fact Hollywood-controlled), quickly came into being, with a redesigned television awards ceremony.

Oscar night, like most things in the peculiar community of Beverly Hills, has a "bottom line." Pretending to be a celebration of this community's *Gemeinschaft,* the Oscar awards are a route to increase dollar turnover, to more *Gesellschaft,* since winning an Oscar can double a performer's market value. The subject of our next chapter is the business life of Beverly Hills.

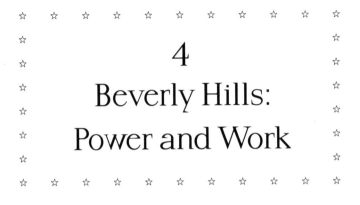

4
Beverly Hills:
Power and Work

In 1979, for the first time, talk-show host Johnny Carson crossed over in true California style and hosted the annual Oscar ceremonies—a job hitherto reserved for a comedian with at least a vestigial connection with the movies. Carson was a great hit. One man did not need reminding. He was Fred Silverman, president of the NBC television network and anointed high priest of American television who had been recruited to get NBC out of third place in the networks' race. Earlier in the year Carson had caused Silverman to intensify his already hectic schedule of trans-America commuting between Beverly Hills and network headquarters in New York. First, Carson used the platform given him as the cover subject of *Rolling Stone* magazine to hint that he was bored. Then he let it be known during a serious interview on CBS that he was planning to leave the *Tonight* show. On Wall Street RCA common stock fell fractionally.

Carson's show was enormously profitable. NBC's revenues from the program were not tremendously high (net, they ran at $190,000 per broadcast in 1979–80). It was a late-night program, after all. But the key figure is the cost of the *Tonight* show, some $59,000 per program. Carson himself was the only major cost, since guests were paid the minimum (union-approved) "scale" rates and the program's staff was small. This made a handsome net income to NBC per episode—$131,000—every weekday night. Since, on these calculations[1] the Carson program was showing a weekly profit of $650,000 in January–February 1980, Johnny Carson had plenty of ammunition with which to bargain.

Fred Silverman set up a heavy battery at Carson's door; threats of legal action for breach of contract alternated with ardent wooing by Silverman, promising financial sweeteners for Carson to stay. By autumn he had so decided: on the basis of a deal worth around $3 million a year for him for a reduced number of shows and including a complex deal between certain of Carson's corporations and NBC over residual rights and future Carson, Inc., productions.

This story may not be inspiring, but it has high illustrative value—here in capsule form is a picture of the new Hollywood. At the top of the pile are the television networks, each part of a bigger conglomerate; but even corporations of such scale as RCA (owners of NBC) may be dependent on a single product for their marginal profit. Just as NBC depends heavily on Carson, so RCA's recording arm grew fat on the music of Elvis Presley, ever since, in 1956, it paid Sam Phillips $35,000 for Presley's masters and back catalog. Presley's death, like Carson's mooted departure, posed problems. Thus the Carson story shows that in the new Hollywood there is a swathe of personal power. Carson is rich enough to leave the *Tonight* show; the musical group, the Eagles, is far too wealthy to be induced into the recording studio to make a new album—to the chagrin of WEA Records (subsidiary of Warner Communications). The relations of Carson and NBC are founded on labyrinthine contracts; numbers, points, and percentages are spattered about. So, too, in Hollywood where "creative accountancy"—the deliberate disguising of complete financial returns, especially from movies—is a new art form.

This chapter is an attempt to map the very special brand of

---

1. Which came from *Variety*, April 30, and June 4, 1980.

California power wielded in and around the media community of Beverly Hills. In Chapter 3 we described the community's Californian culture; here we talk about its controllers and workers. A first point is about the anachronisms that confuse many visitors to Beverly Hills.

Novelist-turned-screenwriter Joan Didion says that she is used to visitors who arrive at Los Angeles International Airport thinking the one thing they know is that the studios are morgues, shuttered up and powerless in a brave new world of independent producers and freelance film-makers.[2] True, there are no longer actors bound hand-and-foot by seven-year contracts; true, also, that there is no longer the old 1930s' cartel with a few vertically integrated companies—producing, distributing, and exhibiting movies in their own theater chains. No longer do a few major companies exhibit each others' films and easily dominate both stars and unions. But the studios live, turned bankers and landlords. Hollywood has, since the 1930s, gone freelance. But in a freelance jungle, those who retain even reduced power are still potent. Moreover some of the old major movie companies are now big in the new fields of television, records, and "software." There is indeed evidence of a kind of cartelization in and between these new fields of entertainment production.

The central question of this chapter is who calls the shots in the Beverly Hills work community? To answer it, we look first at the size and functions of the Hollywood corporations (noting the division between California and New York of ownership and production). But, as the example of Johnny Carson demonstrated, Beverly Hills has created a new kind of personal power. Some of the community's strongest denizens are agents, dealers in points on gross, packagers of talent, salespeople of human skills. There has arisen a new California breed of agent in recent years, and he is (she is, in the case of Susie Mengers) a new potentate. Against the corporations are ranged the entertainment industry's labor unions. We focus on the Screen Actors' Guild—a hybrid organization which acts as an agency for the corporations as well as a representative of the workers and an adversary of those same corporations.

2. Joan Didion, *The White Album*, London, 1979, pp. 155–57.

Louis B. Mayer's Studio Is Dead, Long Live Lew Wasserman's Conglomerate

MGM under Louis B. Mayer in the 1930s was undoubtedly the leading Hollywood studio. Its rapid decline after 1950 is often quoted as an illustration of the fall of the studio system. MGM's production of movies was separated from Loew's lucrative theater interests. Then MGM failed as a maker of motion pictures and of television programs. Under the guidance of Kirk Kerkorian,[3] the company headed for California's out-of-state colony in Nevada and invested in hotels and casinos in Las Vegas, keeping a minimal stake in movies and television. Less well known is the fact that MGM retained much of its Culver City plant, renting it out to other companies. By 1980, MGM was back, making an attempt to build up a separately operated film company under the leadership of David Begelman, a controversial Californian whom we will revisit.

MCA-Universal has been the leading Hollywood company of the television age; its head, Lew Wasserman, was generally regarded in the 1970s as the leading figure in Hollywood, just as Mayer had been forty years earlier. MCA, as we have seen, was originally a major New York talent agency which helped push television westward; in the 1960s it became the major television packaging company. This conjuring trick involved a number of adroit purchases of other companies, and a three-pronged attack on the television business. MCA, as a talent agency, began to put the elements of television shows together, notably their stars. Later MCA moved from merely packaging, to doing the whole production itself. MCA was quick to see television's need for content and thus the significance of old movies. It pounced on several big film libraries at bargain prices.

Through most of the 1970s MCA-Universal appeared to be the ideally balanced Hollywood company—with about one-third of its revenue coming from television production, one-third from theatrical movies, and one-third from other things including recorded music. After MCA's initial move into television production, the U.S. Justice Department forced it to give

3. Dial Torgerson, *Kerkorian*, New York, 1974.

up its by then much smaller agenting business. At this time following anti-trust problems, MCA saw the benefit of cultivating politicians, Democrats and Republicans, both national and Californian. MCA also established an especially close tie with NBC, for some years providing much of its prime-time schedule.

As a self-contained conglomerate, MCA established a tradition of appointing young managers (baby moguls) to senior positions. They got the goods. In the mid 1970s MCA had great success with *Jaws*(1975) and in 1977 produced some sixteen hours of weekly prime-time television output. Three years later, however, this television level was down by half, illustrating that television production—even for the industry leader—can be every bit as cyclical and unpredictable as the making of successful films.

Warner, by the late 1970s had taken the mantle of Hollywood's new leading company. Owned by the Kinney conglomerate, Warner Communications, Inc. (WCI) had been relatively unsuccessful at television but drew about one-third of its revenue from movies and another third from recorded music. This balanced success in both films and records was much admired because Hollywood in 1980—uncertain about the new media future of cable, satellites, pay cable, and discs—felt that, whatever the future turned out to be, it would probably be related to recorded music. Moreover, many believed that Warner—perhaps through its experience in distributing its own semi-autonomous record labels, Warner, Elektra/Asylum, and Atlantic—was a company uniquely able to manage the talents of independent people: it attracted some of the best independent movie-makers to use its production and distribution facilities.

Quadrille: Conglomerates and Indies, Creative Managers and Business Managers

As the careers of the three companies—MGM, MCA, and Warner—show, the majors have a different balance of interest in entertainment. Sometimes, discussions of power and influence do not get beyond a single company's finances or anecdotes about the power plays of a few individuals. But there are com-

mon features in the new Hollywood, with four fairly distinct
levels of companies arranged in a pyramid:

1. The *network conglomerates*—RCA (NBC), CBS, ABC—
are at the top. Each has a significant Hollywood presence in the form of production and office buildings:
Johnny Carson tapes his shows at NBC's Burbank plant.
Their power in Hollywood rests heavily on being the
three major buyers of programing for prime-time television. They have other television interests (such as
owning three local network stations, KNBC, KNXT,
and KABC). CBS and RCA are two of the dominant
record producers in the United States. The networks
also have a wide range of other involvements in old media such as books and new media such as cable.

2. The *Hollywood conglomerates* constitute about nine
companies: MCA-Universal, Warner, Columbia Pictures, Twentieth Century-Fox, MGM, United Artists,
Paramount, Disney, and Polygram. Most of these companies in 1980 had annual revenues of between $500
million and $2 billion, say around $1 billion. Apart from
Polygram (a record major, diversifying rapidly into film
and video), all of the others are descended from old
Hollywood companies. Most are part of larger conglomerates. They belong to Hollywood in the sense that they
own office buildings and some form of major production plant there. New York is more often the corporate
headquarters. These companies distribute nearly all
American theatrical movies that gross significant
amounts; they themselves produce very roughly half of
these movies. These companies (in fact, mainly MCA-
Universal, Paramount, and Columbia) in 1980 produced
about half of all prime-time television. Most of them
tried in the 1970s to get into records in a big way, and
in 1980 Warner, Polygram, and MCA produced about
half of all records sold in the US; CBS and RCA produced a third. The complexities of power in the new
Hollywood are well illustrated by the popular music industry. At its core is the record label, which may be a

regular commercial entity such as Motown Records; or simply a subdivision of a large company created for marketing purposes. MCA Records, for example, produces records on several labels; they are, Bob Siner, president, told us, a means of allowing staff to work together in small groups, largely a "psychological benefit." Thus MCA produced six gospel albums (LPs) in 1980 on its Songbird label. At the same time, it distributed such independent labels as Source and LAX. LAX (L.A. International Records) is a small record production/management/publishing company located across town from MCA on Sunset Boulevard. It has under contract—to produce records for it—a small number of groups, including Blood, Sweat and Tears. It manages others, for example, War, which has a production contract with MCA.

3. The *independent majors*—colloquially "indie majors"—occupy the next step down the Hollywood pyramid. Less powerful and more numerous than those above them, the number varies from about twenty to thirty, depending on definition. These companies differ from all those above them on the pyramid in two vital ways. They do not own production plant and offices but, typically, rent them from the conglomerates to whom they are also beholden for distribution and finance. Second, indie majors are usually specialists, not conglomerates, and their typical size was around $50–$100 million in revenue in 1980—one-tenth or one-twentieth the size of the typical Hollywood conglomerate. The indie majors are largely confined to one medium—be it film only, TV only, or records only; several in 1979–80 were making valiant efforts to spread themselves more widely.

Thus there was a distinct group of indie majors specializing in television—such as Lorimar, Spelling/Goldberg, Tandem, and MTM Productions. There was another group of indie majors specializing in theatrical movies—this rapidly changing field included a bewildering range of companies encompassing film finance, production, and distribution.[4] And yet another group of indie majors specialized in records, such as Motown, A and M, and Chrysalis.

4. Finally, there are the *freelance-independents*, companies which are typically built around a single individual. Some of these—such as Clint Eastwood's—may in some years have revenue as high as an indie major, but most freelance-independents have much smaller revenue. Their ranks are large, with membership changing rapidly, as some individuals give up the struggle, while fresh individuals come forth with their single movie deal, their television pilot, or their new album.

The very difficulty of defining the bottom two steps of the pyramid is itself indicative of the kinds of multiple and unequal relationships that exist between the steps and types of companies. The line between the top two levels is very clear because various federal regulations so insist. But the line between the *indie majors* and the *Hollywood conglomerates* is much less definite. But the indie majors are dependent on the conglomerates for so many things—production personnel and facilities, office space, distribution, financing, advertising—that everyone knows their landlord may fully swallow them at some later date. If they fail they may be swallowed up; and if they succeed the owners of the indie majors may sell out to their landlord for a big capital gain.

Any list of indie majors is likely soon to get out of date, because these companies typically experience a meteoric rise connected with a single project conceived by a single individual. When this project and its inventor (and their respective offspring) cease to be "hot" the company typically declines; and this process, even for successful indie majors, seldom lasts longer than ten years. Desilu, Desi Arnaz, and *I Love Lucy* are an example. Desilu began in 1951 with half an hour of *I Love Lucy* and peaked in 1958 with ten half-hours and two one-hours of weekly television. It then declined and was bought by Paramount. Quinn-Martin, a major success of the late 1960s

4. Dale Pollock, "A New Breed Emerges—Superindies," *Daily Variety*, June 5, 1979.

(with *The F.B.I.* and others), declined in the late 1970s and was eventually sold to Taft Broadcasting. The hot television independent majors of the early 1970s were MTM Productions (with the *Mary Tyler Moore Show* and spin-offs) and Tandem (with *All in the Family* and Norman Lear's distinctive brand of realistic/sentimental comedy). But by the later 1970s the rising companies were Spelling/Goldberg (with *Charlie's Angels* and a similar vein of fantasy/adventure/comedies) and Lee Rich's Lorimar (*Dallas*).

Several of these cases also involve a special relationship with one network—such as MTM's with CBS and Spelling/Goldberg's with ABC. And in some cases (such as MTM) this also involves renting production plant from the network—just as in the movie landlord-tenant relationship. When an indie major is in heat it has enormous power; this is the corporate equivalent of the stellar performer for whom all producers are bidding. Certainly when a record label, a movie independent, or a television indie-major is successful it has conglomerates lining up to distribute its product; certain individuals—such as Norman Lear at Tandem—have used this power to force the network to accept things it would otherwise have rejected or censored. Yet this power is very limited in terms of the quantity of production it generates and the length of time it endures. A major television independent company in its hottest phase may be allowed to skip the usual pilot stage and use a popular episode as the launching pad for a spin-off series; but next season this privilege may well be withdrawn by the network. Similarly, a once successful independent's new film may become part of that 50 percent of indie product which fails to achieve a domestic theatrical release.[5]

Everyone has to gamble, but the lower down the pyramid the gambler is, the worse odds he gets. The networks at the top are analogous to the casino or the bookkeeper. They take risks, but at odds everyone else would like to have. The Hollywood conglomerates also gamble and at only slightly less favorable odds; but their odds are considerably better than the odds of the indie majors down below.

5. "10-Year Diary of Fast-Fade Indie Pix," *Variety*, October 15, 1980.

As new men of power, recording industry executives sometimes appear distinctly vulnerable: Fleetwood Mac spent many
months in the Village Recording Studio in west Los Angeles
and more than a million dollars, before producing the album
Tusk in 1979. Bob Siner of MCA told us that, on sabbatical, he
had once quite seriously counted up all the factors which determine the success of an individual record. He put the number
at 1200. But his corporate boss, Gene Froelich, in charge of the
company's recorded music interests, was more hard-nosed: "we
face no more hazards than Procter and Gamble or Ford—each
quarter's release is a balance of new product and material from
tried and trusted performers." Material is rarely in short supply. One CBS executive to whom we spoke reported that he
gets up to 200 tapes per month sent in from all over the United
States, unsolicited. (Sixty percent "are not even close," he said.)

One of the difficulties faced by the indie majors is that their
success—when it occurs—is too thinly based on one or two key
individuals or projects. The indie majors cannot easily become
conglomerates because that level of the pyramid is already
filled with well-established companies with public reputations,
publicly quoted shares, access to banks for loans, and a tradition of management succession. The indie majors tend to be
one-man businesses built by individuals whose flair does not
extend to consolidating early successes.

There is a distinct difference between the kinds of people
who run the companies at all different levels. The conglomerates—both network and Hollywood—tend to be run by business managers, with backgrounds in finance, law, or marketing.
While indie majors are sometimes run by businessmen from
such fields as real estate, this level of company is more usually
run by creative-managers, such as film, television, and record
producers. The typical leader of a television indie major is a
successful "hyphenate" such as a writer-producer.

This then is the other pair in the quadrille. The struggle
for power in Hollywood is not only between conglomerate and
independent *companies,* it is also between two contrasted sorts
of *managers*—business and creative. The struggle between the
two kinds of managers is not new elsewhere or in Hollywood;
this was the nature of the struggle between Louis B. Mayer and

Irving Thalberg in the 1930s, to name one of many examples. Some business managers (especially lawyers) are able to move across and become creative managers as well. In his apologia after being sacked by CBS, executive Clive Davis[6] reports that he went to the Monterey Pop Festival in 1967 and was bowled over by, simultaneously, the love and flowers and by the prospect of making a lot of money from the comparatively unknown singer Janis Joplin. It was, he says, "a glimpse of a new world." He was right. His visit to Monterey symbolizes the coming together of a new media role, which very shortly became localized within the Beverly Hills occupational community: that of the creative recording industry executive. A tradition was established during the later 1960s of senior executives—in Davis's case coming from a corporate legal background—in close contact with artists. Hollywood music is, Don Zimmerman, executive vice-president of Capitol Records, told us, "a personal relations sort of business." And an industrial structure has evolved to take account of that fact.

Some creative managers become successful business managers. One such is Frank Price, a former television writer-producer who became president of Universal Television and in 1979 president of Columbia Pictures. However, these men are probably the exceptions. And one reason why in Hollywood so many agents have been put into top jobs is that they seem to offer a mix of creative and business skills.

A dramatic example of this conflict occurred in early 1978 when virtually the entire top management of United Artists left to set up a new independent major (Orion) in protest at the corporate management of UA's conglomerate godfather, Transamerica. Two of these top managers, Arthur Krim and Robert Benjamin, were in fact lawyers by background, but they established at United Artists the model of a movie company which provides financing and distribution to independent producers. That they had established excellent rapport with filmmakers was illustrated immediately after their resignations when a protest advertisement appeared in the trade press signed by some sixty film-makers, many of them international

6. Clive Davis, *Clive: Inside the Record Business,* New York, 1975.

celebrities. Transamerica, which bought UA in 1967, reacted to the walk-out by putting a business manager type in as the new UA president.[7]

In 1979 another defection occurred at Twentieth Century-Fox when the three top movie executives, led by Alan Ladd, Jr., left in protest at corporate management policy as exercised by Fox president Dennis Stanfill, a man with a financial management background. Like the UA defectors, the Fox defectors took shelter in a newly formed indie major based at Warner. As in the UA case, it was a protest by film-making executives against the rule of accountants.

Some Numbers Are More Potent than Others . . . and Some Accountants Are More Creative

Hollywood's reputation for flying by the seat of its pants was always exaggerated. Even in the 1930s there were several crude, but effective, numerical indicators. Star mail was counted; so were numbers of fan club members; there were sneak previews with questionnaires distributed. And while the majors owned their own theaters, there was a mass of in-company data on the public's response at the box office.

Special attention is now paid to ratings supplied by Nielsen and Arbitron and to the four "sweep" months of the year (February, May, July, November), when the local stations' audiences are measured while the schedules blossom with hit movies and other enticements. There are various other research services available: TVQ, which ranks hundreds of leading performers for name recognition and public liking and which network executives take seriously; conventional market research national surveys; the showing of recorded television programs to audiences in special research theaters.

The entertainment industry finds itself operating within a series of numerical grids: just as it also operates within a larger corporate world. Put these factors together—the rating services and other "numbers," the power of networks and of conglomerates—and it makes the question of who controls Hollywood

7. Charles Schreger, "Shootout at the UA Corral: Artists vs Accountants," *Los Angeles Times*, Calendar, August 26, 1979.

enormously complicated. Any project or person with a strong following wind of good previous numbers is in a powerful position. The corporate gods—the networks and the conglomerates plus the TV affiliates, the movie theater chains and the record dealers—all bow before strong numbers.

In practice this means that any company which has recently launched three hit television series or three hit movies or three hit records has a seller's market for the fourth. But most are less certain of their market appeal, and thus the power position is also more ambiguous. Nor—as accompanying Table 4.1 indicates—does everything in fact depend solely on Nielsen ratings. This table indicates that ratings alone (the percentage of U.S. households) have acquired their place in the public mind more as a simple symbol (of a more complex set of numbers) and do not have enormous meaning in themselves. The table illustrates that shows with similar ratings can have utterly different levels of profitability. Rating is only an approximate indication even of revenue because advertisers are paying for the character of the audience, and not simply its numbers, and because shows with similar popular appeal may have enormously different costs.

The data illustrate another point. Especially for the network which is running third, as NBC then was, a small number of shows may provide the bulk of a network's profits. In some cases, additional demands by lead actors can easily be met out of the very large profits per episode; but with other only modestly profitable series, additional demands by actors could be enough to push the show from profit into loss. Take the example of *CHiPs*. The table shows that an increase of say $20,000 per episode (almost half a million dollars a year extra) for the salaries of each of the two stars—the sort of figure an agent might demand—would reduce total network profit on the series by 13 percent.

Even in television—the most measured of the media—ratings do not determine everything. Still less so in films and records, which are less predictable or researchable. And consequently in Hollywood, as in many other businesses, even though ratings and researchers are important, accountancy and accountants are more important. Accountants are the butt of

TABLE 4.1 NBC Primetime Shows 1979–80—Revenues, Cost, Profits, Rating

Show	Number of Epi- sodes	Net Revenues per Episode	Program Costs per Episode	Profit per Episode	Regular Season Rating	Primetime Rating Rank
Little House on the Prairie	20	$775,000	$375,000	$400,000	21.5	17
CHiPS	18	574,000	276,000	298,000	21.4	18
Quincy	19	544,000	358,000	186,000	18.4	45
Real People	20	443,000	291,000	152,000	21.8	15
Best of Saturday Night Live	15	391,000	257,000	134,000	14.0	81
BJ and the Bear	19	440,000	317,000	123,000	16.7	57
Diff'rent Strokes	21	279,000	159,000	120,000	20.3	27
Hello Larry	16	210,000	114,000	96,000	17.0	56
Walt Disney	15	694,000	677,000	17,000	17.3	52
Sheriff Lobo	17	390,000	379,000	11,000	17.6	50
Buck Rogers	18	365,000	381,000	($16,000)	16.3	61

Source: Jack Loftus, "NBC's Primetime Profits," *Variety*, April 30, 1980; "1979–80 Regular Series Ratings," *Variety*, June 4, 1980.

many Hollywood jokes, such as this one about "bureaucratic" MCA-Universal: "At MCA-Universal, if you strip off all the tinsel, what would you find?" Answer: "Just more accountants."

"Creative accountancy" is a commonly heard phrase, which summarizes the view of creative workers who are also profit participants that corporate accountants so creatively pad the cost figures as to ensure that there are few profits left for participants to participate in.

Creative accountancy certainly exists, and it has a legal basis. This basis is a standard document, a lengthy Exhibit A which defines what is meant by "profit." Profit participants such as a writer receiving 2 percent or a leading actress receiving 5 percent, must accept the document's definition of profit, one carefully honed over the years by the studio's top legal talent in their employer's interests. Detailed stories published about specific cases[8] make clear how this expanded definition of profit operates. Basic overheads of production are costed at a

8. Charles Schreger, "*Midnight Express* Profits: Gone with the Wind," *Los Angeles Times*, Calendar, October 28, 1979.

high level (in effect, using successful projects to pay off the overheads of previous loss-makers); capital advances from the distributor incur rates of interest above bank lending rates; while these interest charges are ticking up, the profit participants are often made to wait a year or more beyond the initial release date of the film, which in times of inflation means another effective loss. As the movie goes out into release or foreign markets and earns more revenue, it also means new costs, especially advertising. Finally, studios seem to adopt two separate principles of accounting—based both on cash flow and cash commitment—and at each point apply the principle which most favors the studio.

What all this amounts to is that the original agreement is an unequal treaty—the production company is more powerful than the profit participant and draws up an unequal agreement. It is said that the participant always has the option of paying for an audit of the studio's books. This costs around $15,000 and often pries loose substantially more profit for the determined participant.

The point here is that participation in profits (i.e., the net) is less desirable than participation in the gross. Superstars of film and disc do get participation in the gross. This privilege is rarely accorded because only a few reigning superstars have enough personal power to obtain a treaty that is equal.

The New Potentates: Agents

With agents, as with everything else in Hollywood, there is a pyramid. At the top of the pyramid are a few major agencies— such as the two largest, William Morris and International Creative Management (ICM). These two, and one or two smaller agencies such as Creative Artists Agency (CAA), a breakaway from William Morris, specialize in packaging television and movies and in addition handle most of the top actors, directors, and writers.

Also at the top of the pyramid are small highly personal agencies which handle just a few stars or sometimes a single star plus some of the star's immediate supporting entourage. These elite agencies are always merging with and splitting off

TABLE 4.2 A Successful Film Shows a Loss—*Love at First Bite,* statement of participation, March 31, 1980, one year after initial release

GROSS RECEIPTS:	Cumulative to March 31, 1980
U.S. and Canadian film rentals	$15,551,905
Foreign film rentals	3,645,601
Syndication and pay television	150,000
Record and music revenues	75,000
TOTAL GROSS RECEIPTS	$19,422,506
DEDUCTIONS FROM GROSS RECEIPTS:	
U.S. distributor's fees (Filmways)	$3,931,677
U.S. distributor's expenses (including advertising)	5,858,591
Foreign distributor's fees and expenses	1,977,434
Sales supervision fee (7½% of gross receipts, charged by Melvin Simon Productions)	1,456,688
Melvin Simon Productions distribution expenses	540,635
Television residuals	19,500
New-use fees	23,758
Cash cost of production	3,304,661
Overhead fee—10% of production cost	330,466
Completion fee—6% of production cost	198,280
Interest on cash cost of production	757,981
Additional overbudget amount	1,122,794
TOTAL DEDUCTIONS FROM GROSS RECEIPTS	$19,522,465
DEFERMENTS (Paid after production breaks even):	
Purchase of screenplay and literary material	$50,000
Acting fee—George Hamilton	50,000
Executive producers' fee (Hamilton and Robert Kaufman)	100,000
TOTAL DEFERMENTS	$200,000
NET PROFITS (LOSS)	(299,959)

Source: Charles Schreger, "Where's the Scratch from the 'Bite'?", *Los Angeles Times,* Calendar, August 24, 1980.
Note: Gross receipts, one year after domestic U.S. release, were standing at $19.4 million. Box office receipts were probably over twice this amount. Thus despite a box office take of over $40 million, profit participants in a $3.3 million budget movie had received no profit. However, as Schreger points out, subsequent revenues—including foreign sales and television network showings—would ensure them an eventual profit. *Love at First Bite,* starring George Hamilton, was produced by Melvin Simon Productions and distributed in the U.S. by Filmways (initially American International Pictures).

from the few big agencies. Lower down the pyramid are many other agencies, including some which handle interesting rising talents. But both agents and talents are likely to be poached by the big agents. At the lower depths of the pyramid are agents who are getting 10 percent of the earnings of twenty or thirty largely unemployed talents; about 150 of the 225 Hollywood agencies franchised by the Screen Actors' Guild in 1980 were of this bottom-of-the-market kind.

A few agents are famous personalities in their own right, who publicize themselves more vigorously than do most stars. One of these is Swifty Lazar. Another is Sue Mengers, whose list of clients in 1980 included nine directors, twelve actors, and five actresses. Quoting a minimum charge for the acting services of any of her clients, Mengers coined the phrase, "A million is scale now."

Agents are not new; they were already important and powerful in Hollywood in the 1930s. As mentioned earlier, Leland Hayward was instrumental in bringing New York acting talents into Hollywood in the early talkies era. Hayward's partner was Myron Selznick (brother of David), the Hollywood agent who showed that—contrary to previous opinion—the seven-year contract system was vulnerable to aggressive agenting. In the last year of the seven contractual years, Selznick managed to obtain impressive increases for his stars. The Hayward-Selznick agency later merged with MCA, the key to a series of mergers in MCA's rapid rise in the 1940s.

Around 1950 the agents became much more important in four ways. First, the MCA events demonstrated that agents were not peripheral but, in the new rapidly changing conditions, at the very center. Second, after the 1948 court dismemberment of the Hollywood cartel, agents were negotiating ever-escalating salaries, conditions, and percentages for stars. Third, this invention of percentage-of-the-gross for stars went alongside a new ploy by agents. This was packaging movies—a picture's stars, writer, and director all came from the same agency and each paid 10 percent. (In all of this, the high level of postwar taxation not only made the tax-deductible 10 percent commission seem insignificant but also led to the practice of agencies setting their clients up as companies, with much more favorable tax status.)

Fourth, and most lucrative, in the early 1950s agencies began packaging television programs. Here they took 10 percent of the total production cost of the show plus additional commission from any of their own clients put into the show. Repeated thirty-nine times a year this calculation was the star turn of the new agency business. Initially, television packaging was done almost entirely by the MCA and William Morris agencies.

After these dramatic advances of the 1950s, agents were clearly important Hollywood people. Many left the agencies for careers in the networks or the Hollywood majors. The final big advance for agents occurred during the Hollywood film crisis around 1970. Not only were the currently loss-making movie majors being taken over by conglomerates, but at the same time new young managers were given power at the studios. Within a few years every Hollywood major acquired a new president and they were predominantly former agents. The 1970s was the era of the agents. Agents monopolized almost all the top slots in the motion picture division of the new Hollywood conglomerates. Lew Wasserman, the ex-agent presiding over MCA, was not alone.

By 1980 the two top agencies were still William Morris and ICM. Their scale of operations—including offices in New York, London, and other cities—plus the eminence of their clients made them very hard to challenge. It is in the nature of packaging that the packagers must have—and will attract—much of the top talent across the whole range of media skills. Since the Hollywood and network conglomerates depend on star talent—and since they must approach the talent via the agents—it is inevitable that the top network and production executives are in continuous contact with the top agents. And agents are in almost daily contact with their stellar clients.

This gives the top few agencies a range and quality of up-to-the-minute information about forthcoming projects and deals that leave the smaller, lower level agency to chase the minor pickings. Since salaries paid to talent are so uneven, those of the 10 percenters must be also. Successful agents in Hollywood in 1980 were earning $200,000,* and a few superstar agents several times more.

A small group of current agents and former agents have

---

*As a rough rule-of-thumb an agent needs to bring in commission income three times his direct salary cost. Thus a $200,000 agent must generate $600,000 in commissions, or $6 million in client salaries per year.

thus become as an occupational group even more important than the corporate finance specialists in Hollywood. While some of the younger agents are Californians in origin, many of these agents entered show business during the New York television boom around 1950 and later trekked west.

Agents are the butt of bitter humor. The usual resentment over what exactly agents do for their 10 percent is exacerbated by the elevation of agents to the top of the Hollywood pyramid. This resentment during the 1970s fueled several controversies:

ICM was created by a December 1974 merger between the number two and number three agencies—Creative Management Associations (CMA) and Marvin Josephson Associates (MJA). Some people said then, and repeated later, that in such a centralized business as agenting the Justice Department should have opposed a merger of the number two and three outfits.

—Continuing agency commissions on every episode of a television package have become more and more resented. The Writers' Guild was involved in litigation over this issue with William Morris and ICM, and a compromise was reached in September 1976.[9] This whole issue remains one of the most sensitive in Hollywood, and, despite the enormous interest in the launching of new television series, press stories seldom reveal how the packaging is done and who is getting what 10 percents.

—Another hot controversy concerns the respective legal status of talent agents and personal managers in the state of California. Recent legislation favors managers over agents.

Such controversies are inevitable because, in an industry where deal making is central, deal-makers are potent. The work of agents exhibits the paradox of Hollywood—that it is both highly fragmented and highly concentrated. Moreover, as both fragmentation and concentration seem likely to continue, all the signs are that agents (and perhaps others such as personal managers, who perform overlapping functions) will become still more potent.

9. *Variety*, September 15, 1976, p. 1.

Modern Hollywood agents are impresarios of the crossover, the profitable translation of talent and celebrity from one medium to another. They are not alone. A subdivision of one of Hollywood's recent breeds—the recording industry creative manager—is the record executive breaking into film or television.

Recording industry executives now definitely belong to Hollywood—and not merely because all those we interviewed had the trade papers, the *Hollywood Reporter* especially, on their desks. The most successful of the younger generation of creative managers are dabbling in film or promoting their artists and products by means of film. The Eagles, Willie Nelson, Elton John, and Paul Simon are among the singer songwriters whose works are being adapted for the screen. A key figure leading a new generation of crossovers in 1979–80 was Irving Azoff, a young man who had risen to fame and fortune as personal manager of The Eagles. (He manages other artists such as Boz Scaggs.) Azoff had a key role in the packaging of the joint film and album release of *Urban Cowboy* (1980), which brought together a star name, John Travolta, and a soundtrack featuring a great array of salable artists, including Azoff's own people. Azoff co-produced the film; he was, in 1980, a man with considerable personal power.

Inter-personal Power and Performance

July 14, 1977: There is a party tonight at the Beverly Hills home of Irving Lazar. The host is a diminutive potentate, as bald as a doorknob . . . He has represented many of the top-grossing movie directors and best-selling novelists of the last four decades, not always with their prior knowledge, since speed is of the essence in such transactions; and Lazar's flair for fleet-footed deal-clinching—sometimes on behalf of people who had never met him—had earned him the nickname of Swifty . . . Most of the Lazars' guests tonight are theatre and/ or movie people; e.g. Elizabeth Ashley, Tony Curtis, Gregory Peck, Sammy Cahn, Ray Stark, Richard Brooks . . . The senior media still take social precedence in the upper and elder reaches of these costly hills.

One of the rare exceptions to this role is the male latecomer who now enters, lean and dapper in an indigo blazer, white slacks, and a pale-blue open-necked shirt . . . Johnny Carson . . . This pure and archetypal product of the box shuns large parties. Invitations from the Lazars are among the few he accepts. Tonight, he arrives alone . . . greets his host with the familiar smile, cordially wry, and scans the assembly, his eyes twinkling like icicles . . . Heads discreetly turn . . . Even in this posh peer group, Carson has cynosure status.[10]

Fred de Cordova, Carson's producer, recommended we read this Kenneth Tynan piece about Johnny Carson. In addition to flattering its subjects, this piece illustrates the central position of agents in Beverly Hills both socially and occupationally. Here is another example of how "reality" depends on performances—Carson's entrance attracts excitement in Beverly Hills as in Burbank. In Hollywood, power is about what happens face-to-face and what is said ear-to-ear. This is a world of performances, which are not confined to the studio or stage. In this insecure gold rush world performers are only as good as audiences think they are. Current opinion hinges on the last public performance rendered (though this may in fact be a year or two old). Performance in the little power-plays of everyday life matters, too, thus the prevalence of comments about returning or not returning phone calls, the description of power and status in terms of getting particular tables in the currently fashionable restaurants, the endless gossip about A and B parties, and so on.

Agents are central social performers. They must lunch with, dine with, and give frequent parties in order to impress and retain social contact with their clients, their potential clients, and top producers. If a deal falls through at lunch they have a chance of salvaging it at dinner. Social chatter is backed up by innumerable hours of telephone discussion. Beverly Hills may talk to New York at dawn and to London at midnight, but all day long Beverly Hills talks to Beverly Hills. And just as not

10. Kenneth Tynan, *Show People*, pp. 124–25.

getting your calls returned is one sign of status, so getting calls you don't return is another.

Within this endless buzz of rather instrumental chatter, agents—when asked what they do for the 10 percent—claim that they spend much time and effort "positioning" their clients for future deals and projects. This, simply put, involves the agent's insight that social performances are in reality auditions for media performances.

None of this is new. Even in the old studio days, story ideas were presented to MGM's top executives in spoken—not written—form. And Louis B. Mayer, as befitted the man who presided over a community of performers, was no mean performer himself, always ready to throw a fist, a tantrum, or a smile. Among the innumerable anecdotes of Louis B. Mayer there are many that stress his ability—especially when some ungrateful employee was reluctant to sign the next contract—to give a bravura performance, including real wet tears.

In Hollywood, then, performance and inter-personal power plays have always been important. In the currently fragmented state of Hollywood this has become still more so. Thus a certain star refuses to read the screenplay unless it is accompanied by a firm offer of so many million dollars. Thus Francis Coppola, after producing and directing *Apocalypse Now,* remarked that soon the star actor would charge five million dollars for one day's work and also insist the filming be done at his own home. And in such a world, it is logical that top impresarios of performances and deals should be the community's top people— like Lew Wasserman, Irving Lazar, and Johnny Carson, the great cheerleader of front-of-camera discussions about new deals, discs, and projects.

Hollywood Trade Unions: Yesterday and Today

Although Los Angeles's lack of trade unions played the leading role in attracting the movies, by 1940 Hollywood had become very heavily unionized.

In 1915, as the movie-makers were moving to the West Coast, it became apparent that Los Angeles had one great advantage over San Francisco; despite being in the same state, Los Angeles wage rates were about one-third lower. Indeed, San Francisco had a history as one of the most militantly unionized of American cities, as the result of long battles for control of northern California's gateway—the city's waterfront. Los Angeles had remained antagonistic to labor unions. In 1910 some early attempts at organization had been blown a decade or two backwards by the lethal dynamiting (done by trade unionists) of the *Los Angeles Times* building. The *Los Angeles Times* led an anti-union crusade which lasted for the next fifty years.

The bright lights of Hollywood provided a challenge to would-be union organizers. Hollywood was seen as a way of bringing unions to Los Angeles and as a means for unions to establish national prestige. As it turned out, the history of unionism in Hollywood was a jumble of Californian and national concerns, of prestige-seeking, flamboyant gestures, gangster tactics, political extremism (left and right), and the blurring of fact and fiction.

Unions in Hollywood are typical, in that they are both fragmented and centralized. The *Studio Directory* lists 55 separate trade unions, locals, and guilds. But there are only *two* major unions in Hollywood—the International Alliance of Theatrical Stage Employees (IATSE), which alone has twenty-three locals, and the Screen Actors' Guild (SAG), the most important of the talent unions.

Who has won in the labor struggle of Hollywood? On the whole the employers. They were assisted in the early years by the anti-union stance of the local press; during 1930–60 they were aided by gangsters, and by the anti-Communist Inquisition; since 1960 the employers have in practice succeeded in persuading unions to modify their demands because of the threat of "runaway" productions made in Europe. IATSE, an industrial union for the film industry with theater projectionists its key membership element, has since 1960 adopted an extremely "responsible" policy toward pay bargaining in the context of international competition. The real employers—the television networks—take little part in Hollywood labor negotiations. They negotiate with other national unions—primarily NABET and AFTRA,* in the industrial and talent fields. The networks are thus relatively insulated from Hollywood labor disputes since they can use stockpiled episodes, show old movies, and re-run previously shown television episodes. Network advertising sales losses as a result of Hollywood strikes are minimal.

Employers in Hollywood have been better able to resist union demands than they have demands by agents on behalf of stars. Hollywood talent unions continue to call themselves "Guilds": this is not only an historical relic from the 1930s but reflects their artistic ideologies, which, in encompassing the star system and star values, water down union solidarity and militancy.

The history of Hollywood unionism is intricate—especially the period, 1930–60, which saw the great Hollywood Inquisition.[11] A struggle took place on several levels. Here was a fight between left and right. Secondly, and almost more important, it was a struggle between trade unions and employers. Third, it was a public relations battle in which politicians tried to use the Hollywood limelight, and in which one side used (but tried to conceal its use of) professional criminals while another side was indeed in many cases led by Communists (who attempted to mislead both their supporters and their opponents as to their Communist Party membership).

Central to Hollywood's trade union and publicity problems was that while the film industry's ideology emphasized competition for audience appeal, the industry was a cartel where competition was carefully controlled. Trade unions were dangerous for reasons besides making labor cost more. Unions could potentially exploit the extreme vulnerability of the film industry to stoppages of any kind, and they could use publicity to denounce the employers' restrictive practices in employing labor.

A delicate issue in the 1940s for Hollywood was World War II, around which the "Communist Problem" unfolded. In retrospect it is well established that the total number of Commu-

* National Association of Broadcast Employees and Technicians (NABET); and Association of Film, Television and Radio Artists (AFTRA).
11. The next few paragraphs rely heavily upon: Larry Ceplair and Steven Englund, *The Inquisition in Hollywood*.

nists in Hollywood was about three hundred, of whom about half were screenwriters. Communists in Hollywood were indeed powerful in that—through their energy and diligence—they became leaders of the large number of liberal and pro-Russian organizations which blossomed 1942–45 when the United States and the USSR were allies. Hollywood Communists were, however, in another, and more significant, sense completely impotent. Such power as they had—in voluntary organization leadership and in writing movie scripts—was exercised only on behalf of vaguely liberal/populist causes and sentiments of the kind which at the time President Roosevelt and most American voters also supported. The Hollywood moguls at the time did not greatly care how many Communists there were, since the moguls knew that preaching Communist revolution to the southern California electorate or in movie scripts was too absurd an enterprise for anyone seriously to attempt.

However, World War II *was* sensitive in a different way, mainly because Hollywood had such an extremely good time in the war. The scripts, far from carrying Communist propaganda, were drenched with American patriotism and government propaganda. While location filming, star salaries, and other extravagances were cut back, the demand for films boomed; Hollywood experienced lowered costs and increased revenue—a delight indeed, since as recently as 1932 six of the eight main companies had incurred losses.[12] In the war, Hollywood also got even richer through contracts to make government films—which had the additional benefit of filling gaps in the production schedules and thus spreading overhead.

Hollywood labor was attractive to various potential organizers. Among these were the old AFL, which saw Hollywood as a way into the as yet unorganized factories and shops of Los Angeles; later the CIO; later still the Communist Party, which thought that control and influence of the Hollywood labor scene would bring it prestige and publicity; and finally, the mobsters, who could not resist the combination of glamor (sexual and prestige) and vulnerability which seemed tailor-made for the old tricks of extortion, sweetheart contracts, and labor racketeering.

12. Andrew J. Webb, "Filmbiz Recession-Proof?," *Daily Variety*, April 2, 1980.

For some years Hollywood was troubled by labor conflict in which the standard accusations were "Communist" on the one side and "Racketeer" on the other. These accusations were so commonplace that they were one more factor which made the initial assault by the House Committee on Un-American Activities so ineffectual. "Communist" accusations had been blunted by a decade of repetition.

Both accusations, however, had substance. IATSE, the dominant industrial union, was for years run by mobsters, while opposing craft unions (such as the painters) did indeed come under Communist leadership.

There were three main phases in the unionization of Hollywood. In the early years of Hollywood, the theatrical unions came in from New York, and Los Angeles's freedom from unions was shattered. Next the New Deal legislation, especially the Wagner Act (1935), set off a new round of union organization. The talent (notably the actors and writers) now set up their "guilds"; some of the basic crafts were torn between the CIO and IATSE (AFL) but were unionized. IATSE, after some setbacks, hit a winning streak in the late 1930s under the local leadership of a Chicago hoodlum called Bioff (and the national leadership of Browne).

According to John Cogley's account, Willie Bioff at IATSE was closely involved in repeated corrupt deals with the studio heads; in return for an IATSE closed shop first at Paramount (gained by striking the theaters) and later throughout Hollywood, the movie companies in the late 1930s were saved $15 million by the mobsters.[13] In 1941 Browne and Bioff were indicted and convicted of conspiracy and extortion. This was not, however, the end of mobster influence—which was certainly still actively present, for example, on behalf of Warner Brothers in the Hollywood strikes of 1945–46.

The Communist-influenced Conference of Studio Unions (CSU)—which operated in several craft areas—was the main loser in the anti-Communist wave of the late 1940s.

One consequence of these events was that during the period of the arrival of television in the 1950s Hollywood unions

13. John Cogley, *Report on Blacklisting: Movies,* p. 52.

were feeling anything but militant. After so much tilting at political windmills, they largely gave up political activity.

It is remarkable that throughout the 1970s the Screen Actors' Guild had no full-time Washington lobbyist or representative. This despite the centrality of the FCC and other federal agencies in many issues affecting SAG's members. Needless to say the employers never gave up their lobbying activities. The motion picture industry has Jack Valenti—one of the best-known lobbyists in the nation—looking after its domestic affairs at the Motion Picture Association of America (MPAA) and its equally vital export affairs at the MPEA. Mr. Valenti—when we saw him in Washington—told us that in his view it was vital to have a senior lobbyist and for that lobbyist to be in frequent touch both with industry leaders in Los Angeles and with political leaders in Washington. In practice, the Screen Actors' Guild and other unions allow their political lobbying to be done for them by Jack Valenti and other employer lobbyists.

Whether or not the labor relations scene will continue to be so tranquil is one of the key questions for the 1980s. Whether the new media forms are to depend upon entertainment made in Hollywood will depend upon production costs. Existing investment in production plant and the presence of so much talent locally will be strong plus points, but the cost of craft and other labor will be important also.

We do not claim to predict the outcome but we can point to some issues which may worry management:

—Throughout most of Hollywood's history, Los Angeles provided attractive housing, at lowish prices by national standards. However, California's "slow growth" policies of the 1970s have reduced the supply of housing relative to demand and escalated Los Angeles housing prices. In the long run this may escalate union pay demands.

—There were in 1980 already some signs of increased union militancy over participation rights in the new media.

—It is not entirely obvious that the criminal element in Hollywood labor relations (notably the Hollywood moguls' deals with mobsters in the late 1930s and early 1940s) is a thing of the past. The increased significance of the Teamsters on the

Hollywood labor scene, close ties to Las Vegas and gambling, and the activities of Sidney Korshak (see next chapter) are all indications that beneath the surface there could be a labor scandal waiting to explode.

In the meanwhile the relative tranquility of Hollywood labor relations is one of the industry's most remarkable achievements.

Actors and Writers: Identity Problems and Residuals

How powerful are the actors, writers, directors, and producers in Hollywood? The creative "above-the-line" occupation with the most determined labor organization belongs to the writers. The Writers' Guild of America, West, must be about the world's most heavily staffed labor organization. With a total membership of 5000, of whom only about 1500 were fully employed screenwriters, its Hollywood office has some fifty full-time employees. They direct most of their pugnacity at the employers. WGA is the leader in the classic Hollywood game of negotiating residuals, so that the writer of a successful television series ultimately via syndication can earn in total several times the original payment.

The writer is an essential member of the creative trinity. All writers say that "everything begins with the script" in films and television. Most also seem to agree that despite, or perhaps because of, the prominence of writer-producers in television and writer-directors in films, the pure "unhyphenated" writer is in practice the low man on the creative totem pole.

Writing is regarded as very important. A film project in its early days typically consists of nothing but a script or some other written "property" such as a novel, story, or an article. After the script has been written—in both films and television—it is often rewritten (by the television producer or by a film director) or assigned to a different writer or writers; so much so that frequently authorship of both television and films is disputed. Writing is often regarded as too important to be left solely to writers, or solely to one writer.

Writers also do not deal immediately with the main financing—in the way that producers handle package and budget or in the way that directors handle money-on-wheels in the form of stars. Unlike the director, who can be publicized as the wayward genius who directs the superstars, the writer cannot be so publicized as a superstar without the director and star appearing as mere interpreters, and this would mean throwing away too many publicity assets. A fatalistic "we're bound to lose the publicity battles" attitude is one viewpoint which holds writers together. Another is that all writers in both film and television feel a collective loss of control in contrast to, say, the playwright and the novelist. Screenwriting may be compared with journalism since journalistic skills include rewriting and team writing and journalism has thrown up a few writer-celebrities. Being part of a team of sitcom writers, or being a freelance television action-adventure writer, or writing original film scripts, or rewriting novels for TV movies—all of these are quite different tasks. Nevertheless the WGA has done well in getting a wide range of writers to focus their mutual resentments into a disciplined drive for high pay and professional conditions of work. The Guild's leadership has carefully cultivated this basis of common feeling by raising payments for all (all who get work) and making the minimum rate bite in the real market, especially for television writing. In addition, the WGA in Hollywood has in the past adopted an extremely pugnacious attitude toward any members whose loyalty is less than total—notably the writer-producers and the much less militant New York brethren in WGA (East).

The problems and achievements of the Writers' Guild contrast with those of the Screen Actors' Guild.* Stars are few; the pool of under- or unemployed actors is relatively large. The scale of difference between top and bottom takes some grasping.

Every year SAG figures show a few hundred highly paid actors—560 SAG members in 1979 earned $100,000 or over.

---

*We want to thank the following WGA and SAG staff members who gave us their time and also documentary materials: Leonard Chassman, Alan Rivkin, Marge White, Maureen Holden from WGA; Chester Migden, Kim Fellner, Richard Mentzer from SAG. Needless to say, the views expressed here are ours, not theirs.

Another grade of members earn over $15,000 and below $100,000; there appear to be several thousand such actors—but this figure is, for Hollywood, misleadingly high, since many of these "working actors" are earning their middle-range salaries mainly in television commercials and are New-York-based SAG members. The number of Los Angeles members who earned this much in 1979 may have been as low as 1500. This means that roughly 90 percent of Hollywood's 23,000 SAG members earned from screen acting less than a living wage; most of these in fact did not work as actors for more than a small number of days in the year. SAG's elite are the movie stars; the bulk of SAG members' earnings came from television. For many years the highest single source of earnings has been television commercials, with television programing second, and feature films ranking only third as a source.

Hollywood's main television output consists of some sixty series, and even these, typically, only have a small regular cast; since only some of these series run for even one whole season, probably only about 200 actors have security of employment in a television series spanning at least two whole years. A more common form of moderate working-actor "success" in acting is a sequence of separate projects—guest appearances in television series, the occasional part in a movie, television short series, or television movies, plus one or two commercials.

Most common for performers is the kind of experience described by Anne Peters in her study of aspiring actresses: odd jobs and drama lessons, the search for an agent, auditions but not parts, lying about their age, wondering whether to stop "aspiring." Anne Peters points out that these aspirants temporarily continue to find the life attractive.[14] Being unemployed in Hollywood, or waitressing, is better than working in something else—at least for a while.

In addition to the regular actors and stars there are the screen "extras" who have their own guild organization, minimum rates of pay, and so on. In 1980, however, about 75 percent of Screen Extras Guild members were also members of

14. Anne Peters, "Aspiring Hollywood Actresses," in Phyllis L. Stewart and Muriel G. Cantor (eds.), *Varieties of Work Experience*, New York; 1974, pp. 39–48.

SAG, so the proposed merger of SEG into SAG should not make much difference.

The Screen Actors' Guild has had no less than five strikes between 1945 and 1980, which might make it sound like a rather belligerent union. But three of these strikes were about better rates of pay in television commercials. And the 1980 strike—primarily over new media—was to make up for lost time and the depredations of inflation by laying claim to a small slice of the gross in these new fields.

SAG has had to confront two major turning points since its founding in 1933. The first of these, in 1937, did not involve a strike. But the first contract was signed then, and some of the provisions achieved give an idea of how hard conditions were prior to 1937: The contract called for the first minimum rates; 12-hour rest periods between calls; overtime; and a meal break allowed after 5½ hours' work.

The second turning point occurred at the 1960 strike under the presidency of Ronald Reagan. Two very important advances were achieved: a pension fund and a system of payment to actors when theatrical films were shown on television. This still remains a controversial negotiation, with some older SAG members still thinking that Reagan sold them down the river. This was because television payments for early movies were largely forgone—these revenues diverted into the pension fund. The strike lasted six weeks, by which time there were signs of declining support from the membership. Reagan's leadership at this point—and others—appears to have been more farsighted than that provided by most other SAG leaders both before and since.

In the 1970s SAG has seen much internal strife over issues of ethnicity and gender. These issues are real enough. Research shows that ethnic minorities are under-represented on the screen, and so are women—especially women over age thirty. Kathleen Nolan, the first woman to become president of SAG (1975–79), made the Guild much more aware of such issues, but this added awareness led to few other changes and did seem to exacerbate conflict within SAG's membership and staff.

SAG's problems focus upon its enormous membership in

relation to the amount of acting work available. And this in turn relates to television commercials. People become actors in the hope of becoming stars. Only about 1 percent of SAG's members are stars, and about 10 percent of its Hollywood members are "working actors"; but the commercials work is spread more widely, and it is this which both boosts the membership and allows thousands of actors each to earn a few thousand dollars "acting."

Another problem is the impossibility of reconciling the needs and aspirations of millionaire and unemployed members. It needs its few hundred star members for several reasons. It needs the prestige their adherence confers within a star-focused industry; it also needs their dues, which are so arranged that highly paid actors pay ten times the dues of the lowly paid (but even here the Writers' Guild is more tough minded—its percentage of earnings basis meaning that the highest paid writers contribute more than one hundred times the lowest paid).

But SAG, which used in its first twenty years to have mainly stars in its top elected positions, now has few active on its behalf. This is a loss because stars these days often seem to possess both entrepreneurial and—perhaps even more vital—political skills. But they prefer to use such skills directly in politics, while SAG rules do not allow anyone who employs actors (which many stars do as actor-hyphenate-entrepreneurs) to hold elected office.

For the lowly and only occasionally employed actors SAG can do very little. SAG officials claim that the Guild does much for the regular "working actors." But apart from keeping the minima for television commercials in line with inflation, what else does SAG do? Much of its activity goes into policing existing contracts.

The television residuals operation consumes a large fraction of the total staff at SAG's headquarters. Partly because of doubts about the employers' diligence in handing over residual payments for television showings, SAG has taken over much of the industry's bookkeeping work in this field. In the year ending October 1979, SAG processed 122,260 separate residual checks, the average check for $262. SAG also attempts to seek out cases where residuals have not been paid for television shows in particular local markets. This is a costly operation which SAG should not be doing. If the guilds do it at all, SAG should clearly have merged its residual operation with AFTRA's and with those of the Writers' Guild and Directors' Guild. But surely SAG should make the employers bear the cost of paying money which they legally owe to SAG members? And apparently, these days, few major employers are laggard in paying.

What should SAG be doing? One popular answer is that it should merge with AFTRA—the New York-based live (and taped) performers' union with which it has jointly conducted its last two strikes. But AFTRA's elite are the star anchorpersons of television news, and it seems that, at the last moment, these eminent newspersons cannot quite stomach merging with a bunch of mere movie actors. They will eventually.

Something suggested by many outsiders is that SAG should be much more severe in limiting entry. But the SAG reply is that everyone—membership and staff—favor the present system, which says that anyone who can get even one small part in a low-budget movie is entitled to full membership. Another obvious SAG policy would be to move much closer to the other creative guilds—notably the writers' and the directors', since all three are basically trying to increase the creative workers' slice of the pie. But the failure even to merge residuals operations shows how far off a united front is.

Finally, should not SAG direct much more of its effort to political lobbying? The importance of television as well as cable and other FCC-regulated media means that many issues can now be more realistically pursued in Washington than in Hollywood. Moreover, SAG's claimed concern with "improving" (however defined) the content of video entertainment must ultimately depend upon decisions taken by federal regulators and by others on the East Coast such as network censors ("program practices").

SAG's reluctance to lobby in Washington would be inexplicable were it not for the events of the anti-Communist inquisition. To many people in SAG, politics, lobbying, Washington are words that summon up memories of bitter internal disputes to which they do not want to return. The quiescence of the actors' guild—especially in contrast with the actors' agents as a group—is indicative of where power lies in Hollywood.

The Television Series Producer: The View from Sunset Boulevard

The television producer is an example of how publicity often goes alongside non-publicity. Few people outside the industry realize that the executive producer is the dominant figure in series television. Cy Chermak, (executive producer of *CHiPs*, and previously of *Ironside*) noted that whenever a journalist interviewed him the first question was "what does a producer do?". The point about television series (other than those recorded in front of a studio audience) is that each series employs several different directors and several different writers in a single season. The executive producer hires these directors and writers; he also is in overall control of casting and editing; most important, he is in strategic command of the scripts, which is where all the other decisions come together—budget, casting, locations, phasing in new continuing characters.

One reason so few people outside know this is that the series producers tend not to have publicists—they do not need a publicist if everyone in the industry already knows about them and if their reputation does not depend on their personal popularity with the audience. In Hollywood, publicity is something that people seek for a purpose—usually to get more or better work. An executive producer with twenty-two to twenty-five episodes to make in a season already has more than enough work. The producers we spoke to agreed that their biggest tasks were scripts, casting, and editing. Typically, on an adventure series the year's scripts would be written by between four and a dozen different writers and directed by the same number of different directors. Gene Reynolds (executive producer of *Lou Grant* and formerly of *M.A.S.H.*) told us that each of his scripts went through five stages: "A treatment, first and second draft, final in-house polish, which (after an actors' lunchtime reading a few days before the start of shooting) is given a final-final polish."

In addition to these five versions of each script (which is over 100 script versions to read and discuss in total) there is preliminary research. Reynolds said his second biggest amount of time went into casting the non-continuing parts. Casting involved—with associate producer, casting director, and episode director—"reading" actors in the parts for several hours in the week before shooting. The other big task of the executive producer is editing; although the "first cut" contractually is a director's right, in series television this does not mean a lot. Reynolds, like other executive producers, sits in on much of the editing, but not all; he leaves dubbing to an associate producer, and music to a composer.

When Muriel Cantor interviewed producers for her classic *The Hollywood Television Producer* in 1967–68, she found three types of producers: old B movie producer, new film-makers, and writer-producers. Since then the writer-producer has become the dominant type. Evidence for this is that even producers who were not initially themselves writers have now become *writer-producers.*

As elsewhere in audiovisual Hollywood the written word has extraordinary importance. This is illustrated by the various grades of "producer." In some cases the "executive producer" may have more than one show; below the executive producer is usually a "producer," an associate producer, and one or more "script editors." All of these people, however, are likely to be involved as writers or at least in judging the writing of others. In action-adventure series television the dominant hyphenate is the writer-producer. Several of the producers we talked to were really triple hyphenates, since they also themselves directed some episodes.

Action-adventure series television presents various problems. For example, Matthew Rapf described the shooting of *Kojak,* which involved filming exteriors, and using a second unit, in New York City; here a big problem was transferring the New York atmosphere to studio work in Los Angeles. Leonard Katzman described a somewhat similar problem with *Dallas,* which, however, in 1980 differed from other series in having a continuing story line and a "Bible" on the soap opera model. Bert Metcalfe as executive producer at *M.A.S.H.* was slightly unusual in being an actor by origin and having in Alan Alda a star who also sometimes directed episodes. Another unusual aspect of *M.A.S.H.* was its seeking out stories from doctors who had served in the Korean war. Meta Rosenberg, executive producer of the *Rockford Files*, was slightly unusual in being a former agent and having had the star, James Garner, as a client. Asked about the distinctive flavor of *Rockford Files*, Rosenberg—like other producers—traced it immediately to the writers, in this case three in-house writers.

The producers had a few other things in common. All are highly paid and either resent not getting "residuals" or will not admit that they do get them. All worked extremely hard, especially from June to March, when some twenty-three episodes have to be made in about thirty-nine weeks. All lived in the northwest quadrant of greater Los Angeles. The average age was around fifty, and half the producers were Jewish. They were too busy to have, or need, a very big social life. They tended to say that their friends were mainly from television (not films) but did include a few "civilians" such as doctors and lawyers.

Muriel Cantor[15] sees the production of television series as a compromise between many interests—producers, production companies, outside commercial and ethnic lobbies, and federal regulators and the advertisers—with the networks themselves perhaps holding the key veto interest. The television producer is an unknown potentate. But, as with others in Hollywood, his power is limited to a narrow span, although he has a wider significance as one of the main examples of the creative manager species in the new Hollywood.

15. Muriel Cantor, *Prime-Time Television*.

5

The Two Californias

Race and economic power are often missing from the view of California conveyed by the state's media to the world. Absent is the illegal immigrant paid below the minimum wage, fearful of deportation to Mexico, and vulnerable. The scale of illegal Hispanic immigration is only one factor that makes California unusual. California is further set apart by its history of Asian immigration and anti-Asian racism.

The physical layout of California enables people to avoid seeing how the other half lives. The two major cities are so arranged that minority ghettos—in contrast say, to New York—are not close to where rich people work and live. In both the Bay Area and Los Angeles the ghetto may be in a suburb twenty miles away. And in California, suburbs in two different locations in the same city may have quite different climates: if the noon temperature on the coast at Santa Monica or Malibu is 75° F, inland in Hispanic east Los Angeles it may easily be 100°. The media cater to, and cover, only one of the two Californias. The other California remains largely invisible.

Hispanics

"Television and the media are the last bastions of racism in the United States." The judgment of Danny Villaneuva, general manager of KMEX-TV in Los Angeles, is terse and sums up a belief held by Hispanics that they are deliberately excluded from the media spotlight. It is a view held by blacks, too. For example, in 1977 the NAACP wrote to the Federal Communications Commission opposing the license renewal of all three of the network-owned Los Angeles television stations: too few blacks were hired; too few appeared on camera.

Villaneuva, a controversial figure even in his own community, is telling us about the exclusion of Mexican-Americans from the fruits of California media capitalism. He is no critic of such talismans of media objectivity as audience measurement. But the ratings organizations cannot or will not measure us, he claims, referring to his UHF Spanish-language station. Since the ratings book is the bible of the advertising agency time buyer, television advertising either passes us by altogether or we get paid for only a fraction of our real audience. Even though 44 percent of kindergarten-age children in Los Angeles have Spanish surnames, KMEX gets no baby food advertising. The annual purchasing power of Los Angeles Hispanics was estimated at about $6 billion in 1980. Villaneuva claims that 81 percent of Mexican-Americans in Los Angeles are regular viewers of his station. "The consumption figures will blow your mind," he says.

The Hispanic population of California is demographically visible to the Anglos; but in terms of Anglos' everyday experience and media consumption, invisible. Most Californians are aware of the "illegal alien problem"—politicians seeking votes prefer to say "undocumented aliens." To some in California the border patrolmen of the federal Immigration and Naturalization Service are latter-day heroes attempting to hold back a remorseless and illegal human tide. In San Diego County alone in 1979, some 338,681 people were apprehended crossing illegally into the United States; many more probably succeeded. Wealthy families from Marin County to La Jolla benefit from the "problem" by employing for low wages Hispanic maids, cooks, gardeners, and swimming pool cleaners without looking too closely at their civic status. The restaurant business and the clothing industry in Los Angeles depend for their very existence on labor paid below the legal minimum. Such facts can be discovered by the diligent newspaper reader. But mostly they remain invisible. Along the freeway, or on television, you will see few Hispanics.

Meanwhile, in the 1970s the county of Los Angeles acquired a minority majority.[1] Estimates of the Hispanic population are notoriously unreliable in that illegal immigrants are understandably not keen on being counted. Everyone agrees that the 1980 Census undercounted the real number of California's Hispanics—they disagree only on the scale of the undercounting. We were both among the thousands of foreigners in Los Angeles on Census day who dutifully completed the forms. One complaint in California was that the Spanish language forms used official Spanish, which many Mexican-Americans had difficulty in understanding.

Mexican peasants have labored in the Central Valley for many years bringing in cash crops. But Ted Fritts, owner and executive editor of the *Bakersfield Californian*, describes the surrounding county of Kern as effectively segregated. "There is absolutely no crossing of racial or cultural lines," he told the *California Journal:* "Many prominent businessmen here literally deny the existence of blacks and Mexican-Americans. Their problems don't exist because they don't exist."

What this invisibility means was aptly summed up in an off-hand remark made a few years ago by the publisher of the *Los Angeles Times*. Of his paper's coverage of, and sales to, the Hispanic community—which has, incidentally, now swallowed up the downtown section of Los Angeles where the *Times* is headquartered—Otis Chandler said: "It's not their kind of paper. It's too big, too stuffy, and if you will, too complicated." The ambiguity of the statement accurately reflects the *Times*'s attitude of strained boredom with (rather than overt prejudice toward) Los Angeles Hispanics.

Hispanic invisibility is a product of language differences.

1. Tony Quinn, "The Transformation of LA from an Anglo to a Minority City," *California Journal,* June 1980.

Hispanics are the only large American minority who have "got away" with bilingualism. Two theories obtain. One is that because of the continuing refreshment of Spanish—from neighboring Mexico (and also from the rest of Latin America and the Caribbean)—the dominance of English will be diminished. In California there was some evidence—especially in the late 1970s—that this was starting to happen in the media. KMEX is only one of the stations linked via satellite to a Spanish international network, which allows it and other Spanish-language television stations in Fresno and the Bay Area to fill their airtime with soap operas and films supplied from Mexico City.

Another sign that the Hispanic media of California were breaking out of their cycle of marketing deprivation was the comparative success of *La Opinion,* the sole Spanish language daily newspaper in Los Angeles. For five decades since the 1920s *La Opinion* struggled, a small obscure immigrant daily. But in 1975 its publisher, Ignacio Lozano, Jr., installed a modern offset press. Between 1975 and 1980 circulation doubled—the greatest increase of any daily newspaper in greater Los Angeles in those years. A glossy magazine, *Imagen,* has also been successfully launched.

The other theory—believed by some Anglo newspaper editors—holds that as Hispanics settle and get richer they will go the American way and read English-language papers. Tom Kirwin, editor of the *Fresno Bee*'s editorial page, put versions of both theories to us. His paper is one of the McClatchy chain, three surprisingly liberal daily papers in Sacramento, Fresno, and Modesto owned by an old Sacramento family. Recently, recognizing the growth of Hispanic numbers in the Central Valley, the *Fresno Bee*'s editors experimented with a Spanish-language supplement—a one-page résumé of the news every weekend. It lasted six months. It annoyed the paper's regular Anglo readers who, like most Californians, bitterly oppose bilingualism. It also failed to attract Hispanic readers. Probably some would never have read such a comparatively up-market paper as the *Bee* anyway; others were offended by the "ghetto" offered their language. So now the *Bee*'s editors are confused. All they know is that, despite having self-consciously recruited Hispanics to their reporting staff, the affairs of La Raza are a closed book to them. Also that newsstand sales of the paper in the heavily Hispanic downtown of Fresno are poor and that—as the Hispanic ghetto increasingly encompasses more of Fresno—the *Bee,* like other Californian dailies, faces the prospect of one day having few readers inside its base city.

Nowhere have California Hispanics been traditionally less visible than in the fields. From World War II until 1964 "bracero" programs brought gangs of Mexican laborers into the fields for the harvesting season—with buses to transport them out again once the crops were harvested. Occasionally a crusading journalist would descend on the fields and win a Pulitzer Prize for his emotion-stirring stories about the shocking conditions in which they worked—as Stanton Delaplane of the *San Francisco Chronicle* did in the late 1940s. But no paper of the major California cities gives agriculture sustained coverage. Few papers have agricultural correspondents. The *Fresno Bee* alone of California newspapers gives farming and, especially farm labor, adequate coverage—and it is writing for a community dependent on agriculture. Television's coverage is skimpy. In a year's viewing of Bay Area and Southland television neither of the authors got more than the flimsiest information about the state's agriculture—and that despite the important strike by farm labor against lettuce growers in spring 1979. (Like many strikes before, this one also involved a murder.)

It was the *Fresno Bee* which first covered the activities of Cesar Chavez—founder of the National Farm Workers' Union in 1962 (after a subsequent merger, the UFW)—and favorably enough to win the paper's editors the enmity of local grower interests. Don Slinkard, editor of the *Fresno Bee,* admitted to us that his paper's monopoly allowed the liberal McClatchy family to weather the withdrawal (and threatened withdrawal) of advertising by farming companies in the Central Valley. Chavez enjoyed a moment in the national media's spotlight with his organized boycott of Californian grapes; but he and the UFW have retreated into the shadows, lit only occasionally. During the 1979 lettuce strike the growers bought full-page newspaper advertisements warning that "this time" Chavez and the UFW had gone too far. Chavez in turn appears on camera for a once-in-a-while demonstration to utter threats about wresting back for the Mexicans the land they once "owned" (a claim without the slightest legal or historical basis).

Indeed, although California's early major landowners were Spanish and Mexican, most of today's landless Mexicans are quite recent arrivals. The settlement of California by white Americans in the nineteenth century coincided with the genesis of a particularly virulent strain of racism directed eastward across the Pacific against the Chinese and later the Japanese. Institutional racism persisted well into the twentieth century. From its birth until the 1940s the California press was roundly anti-Asian. C. K. McClatchy, the legendary founder of the *Sacramento Bee*, attacked trusts and Chinese immigrants with equal venom. The state's paranoid racism boiled over after Pearl Harbor in December 1941. California's Japanese were interned, whereas those in Hawaii were not; an action unnecessary for either strategic or political reasons, which remains a permanent stain on the reputation of the California press (which demanded stern measures) and of the state's then attorney-general, Earl Warren, later hailed as a liberal when Chief Justice of the United States.

But California's Asians have voted white. By and large they have attained—in the case of the Japanese, surpassed—the earnings of whites. In white eyes they have, since World War II ended, faded into the sun-tanned California background. The Japanese ancestry of Senator S. I. Hayakawa hardly mattered in his 1976 election to the United States Senate. Hollywood has toyed briefly with the injustice done the state's Japanese in such films as *Bad Day at Black Rock,* or more recently through comic invention in the the film *1941.*

Asians now fit in as part of the colorful backdrop the state provides tourists and media-watchers. San Francisco's Chinatown, actually a low-income ghetto, has the charm of a movie set; Los Angeles's Chinatown gave a recent film its name, but in it the Chinese were merely extras in a white man's drama. A small Chinese-language press lives on, strengthened by satellite hook-ups which now allow two-center printing in New York and San Francisco. The Vietnamese arrivals of the 1970s have become another invisible minority—except where many have settled in the old rundown districts of Hollywood.

But the Hispanics are the great unassimilated. Despite the efforts of Governor Jerry Brown, the Hispanics have low rates of voter registration. No Hispanic sat as a city councilman in Los Angeles during our sojourn there. In Orange County in 1978, Hispanic voters could not prevent two of the first-ever Hispanic judges being turned out of office. To a media manager such as Danny Villaneuva, non-participation on the part of Hispanics is a matter of cause and effect: no media coverage, no interest shown. He claims that when the news team from KMEX arrives in the barrio of east Los Angeles to cover a story, the people cheer.

Appearance on television is the crucial symbol of emancipation. But Los Angeles had, in 1980, no Hispanic anchorperson on its major local news shows. Major stations had blacks at their news desks; two star anchors were Asian women, who score on gender, ethnicity, appearance (and apparent intelligence) combined. Perhaps KNBC and KNXT take their lead from the community toward which they as stations are pointed—the Beverly Hills entertainment and media community. That world and the fictive world it produces remain lilywhite (if no longer Anglo-Saxon Protestant). *Lou Grant* has no black or Hispanic reporter in its news room, but maybe that is merely an accurate reflection of the *Los Angeles Times* and of MTM Productions, the company that produces it. By 1980, however, there were a few signs that Hispanics were starting to arrive. At least one would-be comedy series *Chico and the Man* ran in the mid 1970s with Hispanic participants.

For Hispanic parts, Puerto Rican and Cuban actors have often been preferred to Mexicans. After all, "Mr. Lucy," Desi Arnaz, was a Cuban who in the fictional world of *I Love Lucy* managed to impregnate Lucille Ball without offending the Daughters of the American Revolution. But local Hispanic flavor has crept into recent feature films and television entertainment. The popular lead of the television series about the life and flirtations of the California Highway Patrol *CHiPs*, Erik Estrada, looks and sounds Latin (he is actually Puerto Rican). The 1979 film *Boulevard Nights* was shot on location at the junction of Whittier Boulevard and McBride Avenue in inner Los Angeles, and wove its plot around the southern Californian car culture adopted wholeheartedly by Hispanic youth. Other films soon followed, focusing on the east Los Angeles barrio and on illegal border crossings. The bio-pic of Cesar Chavez has yet to be made, however.

At some point in the future of both California media and politics, Hispanic numbers must count. But meanwhile the Hispanics are invisible, especially compared with the state's less numerous blacks.

Panthers and Wattstax

California in 1970 had 1.4 million blacks. Like New York, California is the home of slick black imagery. Its blacks include Huey Newton (founder of the Black Panthers) and Angela Davis. It is now the home of Berry Gordy, removed from Detroit, founder of Motown Records. California is where *Wattstax* played, and where the S.L.A. "liberated" Patty Hearst. Several blacks have been elected to the U.S. House of Representatives from California. Before his defeat by Mike Curb in November 1978, Mervyn Dymally was the state's undistinguished, but black, lieutenant-governor. A black ex-Los Angeles city policeman, Tom Bradley, was elected and re-elected mayor of the city in the 1970s.

The *San Francisco Examiner* claims the best non-white hiring record on the West Coast.* In 1979 it had 23 non-whites on a staff of 200, and most were black. KTVU in Oakland had a black anchorman; most of the leading stations in Los Angeles feature black faces prominently during the evening news. After long years of battling, there are now a few black craftsmen members of such entertainment unions as IATSE. Few of the full-line record companies based in Los Angeles do not have a black executive, even if his only job may be to hold the hands of the black artists on the company's soul music roster.

It sounds like a story of progress. If so, then it has much to do with the explosion of black violence which erupted in Watts

*See table.

TABLE 5.1 Newspaper Employment of Minority Journalists 1979

Newspaper or Chain	Number of Journalists Total	Minority	Minority Journalists (percent)
Miami Herald*	320	51	15.9
San Francisco Examiner	200	23	11.5
Washington Post	353	35	9.9
Los Angeles Herald-Examiner	135	12	8.9
New York Times	670	40	6.0
Knight-Ridder chain	4,762	287	6.0
United Press Internat.	857	52	6.0
Newsday	319	18	5.6
Gannett chain	2,715	147	5.4
San Diego Union	140	7	5.0
Los Angeles Times	572	28	4.9
Boston Globe	330	16	4.8
Chicago Tribune	430	19	4.4
Ottoway chain	492	5	1.0

Source: *Columbia Journalism Review*, March-April 1979, p. 26. This table extracts from the CJR table employers of 300 or more journalists and includes all those in California.
*Includes 30 Hispanic employees of a special Spanish-language section.

in August 1965 which left thirty-four dead and $40 million in property damage. Watts is a world away—but only ten miles down the San Diego freeway—from Beverly Hills. Poverty in southern California is hidden by palm fronds and azaleas, but it is real enough. Compton, the black community next door to Watts, is rated one of the poorest communities in California, with an average income per head only just over half that of California at large.

Blacks first arrived in California in large numbers during and after World War II. They came to work in the new aircraft factories, in munitions, in the new manufacturing industries created by federal spending on the demands of war. Discriminatory housing restricted them to particular communities: to Hunter's Point in San Francisco, to Richmond and Oakland across the Bay, to Watts, Compton, and Vernon in Los Angeles. In 1960 the black baseball star Willie Mays was railroaded by white neighbors out of a San Francisco neighborhood. In 1964, state Proposition 14 effectively legalized the racial discrimination practiced by Californian realtors. This proposition was later ruled to be unconstitutional. But not before Watts caught fire in 1965. Blacks suddenly ceased to be invisible. An army of television reporters and camera crews relayed across the United States images of race war in the sun-kissed streets. More important, it convinced the anguished liberals of the Beverly Hills entertainment community—many of them Jews intensely conscious of oppression—that blacks should be brought in. The connection between Watts (1965) and the appearance on television of black actors and actresses in such shows as *Sanford and Son* (1972–77) is close; and it has much to do with the geography of southern California.

The lesson of Watts for the blacks of California was that media imagery was mutable. The Black Panthers, founded in Oakland, lived and died in the blaze of live television coverage. A splinter group survived into the 1970s and called itself the Symbionese Liberation Army. To its members' imaginations, media meant power: they did not hesitate to choose the daughter of the most powerful man on their horizon, the media magnate Randolph Hearst.

Watts was also a catalyst in the editorial life of the *Los Angeles Times*. Eight years later, the city of Los Angeles elected its first black mayor with the *Times*'s blessing. Even though Tom Bradley's opponent was one Samuel Yorty, a longtime enemy of the *Times*'s editors, this was a revolution. And support for Bradley's black political establishment has continued. Local observers claimed in 1980 that the paper's continuing support of the Bradley regime at City Hall had allowed it to ignore several dubious property deals in the central city in which Bradley cronies had been involved. Hollywood, too, made *Shaft* and *Wattstax;* and *Variety* coined the term "blacksploitation." Richard Pryor and Bill Cosby got serious acting roles. The soap-opera antics of a black family *The Jeffersons* made prime time.

But was the rise of *Sanford and Son*—Norman Lear's adaptation of the British series *Steptoe and Son* into blackface—a harbinger of real change? Aren't blacks, street blacks, poor blacks still largely invisible in the California media? In the fictional world of films and television produced in California, racism in jobs and housing is scrubbed almost clean away. "For all one could gather from viewing television," said the NAACP in 1977, "black life in the USA is a caricature." The increase of black programming after Watts did not continue in the 1970s, and the number of series TV shows with a black presence has altered little since. This is all the stranger in view of the unprecedented audience ratings of *Roots* (1977) as a mini-series on ABC. Carleton Goodlett, publisher of the San Francisco *Sun-Reporter* group of black newspapers, says that television stations move blacks around within their organizations in order to give the illusion that they are employing sufficient numbers. Goodlett's papers give black journalists training they would never get elsewhere, he says.

Blacks still largely remain on the down side of the California dualism. At its crudest the haves are predominantly white, and they have it. Hal Evry, a political campaign manager from southern California, was quoted in the *California Journal* on how to win campaigns in the 1980s: "If you talk to poor people or non-voters you are wasting your time." For "poor" read black and Hispanic. And Watts—fifteen years after the events of 1965—actually seemed worse off in two respects: unemployment and conflict between blacks and Hispanics moving into the area.*

The Police and Minorities

We saw in the last chapter how California's police, its highway patrol and the San Francisco and Los Angeles police departments in particular, were one of its most visible media attributes. They are widely admired by police forces across the nation and have been the subject of innumerable films and television series. The people of Watts went in for widespread looting of television sets during the riots of 1965; but they did not see the Los Angeles Police Department as quite so perfect. Studies commissioned after the riots showed conclusively that many hated and feared the LAPD, especially its chief, William Parker.

* These were among a long list of chronic problems identified in a series of *Los Angeles Times* articles published in August 1980, looking at Watts fifteen years after the riots of 1965.

For sixteen years, from 1950 Parker was chief of police, and during most of that time was the most celebrated cop in the country, with a dazzling reputation in Washington for militant integrity and scientific policing methods. He was also the man who used terms like "the wild tribes of Mexico," and who during the Watts riots appeared on nationwide television talking about ". . . monkeys in a zoo . . . throwing rocks." The taint of racism has lingered. A major controversy in 1979 concerned a middle-aged black lady who refused to pay her domestic gas bill; when two policemen came to her home in south central Los Angeles she threatened them with a knife, and they shot her dead. As Chief Parker before him, the new police chief Daryl Gates (like Parker a virtuoso self-publicist) did not temper defense of his organization with justice. The *Los Angeles Times* acted true to form, too. It initially failed to report the story—despite its importance in the minority community—then it entered the story to point out that the dead woman's name had been misspelled. Later the story got the full *Los Angeles Times* multi-column treatment. Black visibility is still a problem.

The Social Geography of the News

The local television news for Los Angeles illustrates how some people and areas are highly visible while others are largely invisible. The northwest quadrant of greater Los Angeles—which includes Beverly Hills and surrounding communities, plus the white middle-income San Fernando Valley—receives a disproportionate share of television news coverage. But the south and eastern areas, where the blacks and Hispanics predominate, receive little coverage.

Our study involved looking at two hours of evening news on the three Los Angeles network stations for three weeks in April-May 1979.* The northwestern bias of the news came out in several ways. Of 797 stories which had a specific geographical location in Los Angeles the northwest segment with approx-

*We are grateful to the three students at the University of California, San Diego, who conducted this study. Laurie Weinstein, Dale Hagen, and Bob Rubinyi together logged 90 hours of news (3 weeks × 5 weekdays × 2 hours each day × 3 stations = 90), April 23–May 11, 1979.

imately 20 percent of the population received 32 percent of located stories; all of the other outlying areas with together about 70 percent of the population received 35 percent of the television news coverage. The northwest quadrant, on a population basis, received over three times as much coverage as the other outlying areas (which include affluent Orange County).

The social geography of the news is highly selective. For example, within east Los Angeles well over half the stories came from the mainly Anglo areas (Pasadena, Glendale, San Bernardino, and Riverside) and not from the heavily Hispanic areas (such as El Monte and West Covina). This selectivity was even more noticeable within the large southern segment of Los Angeles; it received 10 percent of all located stories, but most of this news was of predominantly white sections along the south coast such as Long Beach and the exclusive white coastal community of Rolling Hills. The entire area of Watts and Compton with a black population of about one million people received only 1 percent of all located stories in Los Angeles. The northwest (with about twice the population) received 32 percent of coverage. Thus on a population equality basis, the northwest received about sixteen times as much TV news coverage as did the black areas of Compton and Watts.

Within the northwest segment also it was the more affluent areas (especially Malibu, Westwood, Sherman Oaks, Encino, and Burbank) which got most coverage. The most concentrated coverage of any single story—10 percent of all located stories over a three-week period—focused on the single event of a rockslide on the Pacific Coast highway in the famous beach community of Malibu. This is a local road; the story emphasis was heavily upon the risk to the expensive beach houses and the inconvenience to wealthy and "celebrity" residents. The story is quick to get; it fits neatly into the definition of what makes a lively story in Los Angeles. All the visual elements are easy to identify. The quick opening shot is of the beloved palm-lined seashore, before the camera swings round toward the rock slide menacing the "expensive homes" below.

There was one other big category of located stories—34 percent came from downtown Los Angeles. These stories focused on institutional sources of news such as City Hall, police headquarters, and courts. A few minority faces on the TV news belonged to politicians, but blacks and Hispanics were most likely to appear in these downtown items as the "suspect" or the accused being bundled into or out of court. Minorities also appeared as "the problem" in downtown stories about welfare or immigration.

In the areas where they live—when they behave non-violently—the black and Hispanic communities receive very little news coverage. The reason is not prejudice, but the relative costs and benefits of covering different stories. News managers try to get two or more usable stories out of each camera crew each day. Downtown and the northwest segment—which together accounted for 66 percent of all located stories—have two major advantages. First, they provide plenty of stories easy to collect; they do not involve hunting about for the story in a potentially hostile neighborhood. Second, the northwest and downtown are close to where the major television stations KNBC, KABC, and KNXT have their offices. KNBC, which is in Burbank, had even more Burbank stories than did the other two.

Another Minority—the Jews

Southern California has had an active strain of anti-Semitism. Not until after 1960 were the Jewish leaders of the entertainment industry fully accepted into Los Angeles "society." The media people of Beverly Hills, despite having been socially acceptable to European royalty and the like for several decades, were still socially unacceptable in such suburbs as Pasadena, where the city's social elite lived. San Francisco was quite different—there Jews had long been well established, socially, in business, and in politics. In San Francisco the Chinese and Japanese were the scapegoats.

The Jews who came with the movie industry to Los Angeles stemmed from New York. As Irving Howe says, they were energetic young men attached to an industry they could enter at the beginning:

. . . Samuel Goldwyn, Louis B. Mayer, William Fox, the Warner Brothers, the Schenks, the Selznicks, Harry Cohn, Jesse Lasky, Adolph Zukor—all followed pretty much in Laemmle's footsteps . . . they were on the lookout . . . for a key to wealth and power.
They found it in the nickelodeon . . . It was a business that appealed to them: strictly cash, a minimum of goods and apparatus, and brand new. A bright young Jew could get in at the start without having to trip over established gentiles along the way. . . .
The Moguls were mostly semiliterate men, ill at ease with English, but enormously powerful in their intuitive grasp of what American—indeed international— audiences wanted. They were soon dining with heads of state, traveling among the international set, winning and losing fantastic sums at Monte Carlo, realizing their wildest personal fantasies, satisfying their every whim, amiable or sadistic. The marks of immigrant Jewishness remained on their every feature and every gesture, and the shrewder among them made no special effort to erase these marks. . . .
Often vulgar, crude, and overbearing, they were brilliantly attuned to the needs of their business. . . . Trusting their own minds and hearts, shrewd enough not to pay too much attention to the talented or cultivated men they hired, the Moguls knew which appeal to sentiment, which twirl of fantasy, which touch of violence, which innuendo of sexuality, would grasp native American audiences.[2]

Yet, in the 1920s and 1930s, while club doors in Los Angeles County were still barred to such men, California opened up to them. William Randolph Hearst, star-struck by Marion Davies, carried the cream of Beverly Hills off to San Simeon, his enchanted castle. Louis B. Mayer, the greatest of moguls, was an enthusiastic Republican, holding several high positions in the party at state level.

Jewishness never died as an issue. One reason was the great fear engendered in the Beverly Hills occupational community

2. Irving Howe, *The Immigrant Jews of New York*, London, Routledge and Kegan Paul, 1976, pp. 164–65. (Published in the United States as *World of Our Fathers*.)

in the 1940s by the anti-Communist inquisition, which only ended in the early 1960s. Anti-Communism in Hollywood had anti-Semitic elements. Part of the attack from the House Committee on Un-American Activities took the form of "American" sneering at "foreign sounding" names. As we have seen, recruits to Hollywood were always tempted to rewrite their non-California past, and the anti-Communist fear gave them added cause. Liberal leaders such as Melvyn Douglas (previously Hesselberg) were repeatedly taunted about their name changing; the insinuation was that changing from a Jewish-sounding to a WASP-sounding name (which in fact was usually done on the urging of the studio publicity department) involved some undercover political motive. There was also heavy insinuation about un-American birthplaces—a sensitive point indeed, since several prominent Hollywood executives had been born in Russia.

Most of the Hollywood Ten (who refused to answer questions about their past and so were jailed) and many of the Communist screenwriters were Jews. The highly conservative climate of southern California contributed to nearly all Hollywood Communists keeping secret their membership in the Communist Party. In the eyes of eager anti-Semites, Jews became doubly suspect. The fact that most (but not all) of the Communist writers and directors and most (but not all) of the reigning studio moguls were Jewish gave the whole Hollywood Jewishness question its peculiar in-grown, but publicly unspoken, savagery: Jew persecutes Jew.

During the 1960s the proportion of Jewish residents in Beverly Hills itself fell below 50 percent. But the "Jewishness" of Beverly Hills still lingers on as a subterranean issue that sometimes surfaces in a code word, sometimes in a conspiracy theory, sometimes in crude anti-Semitic insult. Recently, local black organizations in Los Angeles, including the NAACP, have alleged that blacks are kept out of entertainment industry roles because of Jewish peer group influences. As local Hispanics knock on the doors of Beverly Hills and ask for acting parts, craftsmen's jobs—and their knocks must inevitably get louder—they, too, may scapegoat the Jews.

Meanwhile the "real" southern California Jewish community evolves in a fascinating way. The San Fernando Valley, just to the north, is the main area in California where the Jewish vote is significant; however, in recent years this vote has become less "Jewish" in the sense that it has tended to swing away from Liberal-Democrat positions and into more centrist positions. Will the visibility of this California minority be allowed to decline even further?

Californian Land—the Invisible Valley

When people in Los Angeles talk about "the Valley," they are referring to the San Fernando Valley, the sprawling urbanized tract just north of the Hollywood Hills. But California's valley, secret in many ways, is the Central Valley: 450 miles long, from Redding in the north to below Bakersfield in the south, surrounded by coastal mountains and the Sierra Nevada to west and east, forest and desert to north and south. It produces nearly 10 percent of United States farm output, and in each area the farming is highly specialized; for example, rice around Sacramento, grapes for raisins around Fresno. The land is intensely cultivated and the farming highly mechanized, but certain crops still depend on stoop labor—by Mexicans. The few settlements are tucked away; their names betray their origin. Take Coalinga—named for the Southern Pacific railroad's depot at coaling station A.

For fifty years, from the 1860s till World War I, the history of California was largely the history of the Southern Pacific Railroad. The railroad, likened by novelist Frank Norris to an octopus spreading its branch lines like tentacles across the Central Valley, ran newspapers, ran politics, and ran the agricultural economy in the years when wheat replaced gold as the state's main harvest. Such railroad men as Collis P. Huntington in the south and Leland Stanford in the north founded institutions and dynasties that influence California life today. The great railroad gave California three things. By the beginning of the twentieth century, revulsion against the Southern Pacific's manipulation of politicians built to such a peak that a progressive administration led by Hiram Johnson was elected to Sacramento to implement a program of political reforms that well-

nigh killed political parties in the eastern mould for a quarter
of a century. California's peculiarly weak parties—and the cor-
respondingly strong influence in politics of the state's media—
show the results of these reforms today.

The second residue of the Southern Pacific's pioneering
trail into California is the pattern of land-holding that charac-
terizes the Central Valley and hence the state's agricultural production. It is a pattern of large-scale ownership that is common
to all Californian capitalism: the rapid emergence of the big
studios with their cartel-like arrangements for the production
and distribution of film merely conformed to Californian type.
Southern Pacific, an agent in the disbursement of federal land
in the state, had a stake in large-scale ownership. To this day,
the company owns large parcels of California land: a total of
3.8 million acres in California, Nevada, and Utah.

The Southern Pacific bought the first railroad laid into California from the east, by the Central Pacific. And the SP continued a tradition of the Central Pacific: the third legacy it has left
for the modern corporate California. This was the intimate relation between private power—the company—and a grant- and
money-dispensing government. The Central Pacific had to be
bribed by the federal government to lay its tracks west. Likewise the Southern Pacific in a gigantic land scam secured the
rights to millions of acres of salable arable land from the government as its price for constructing a north-south railroad in
California in the 1870s. The tradition has stuck. Modern California capitalism is a handmaiden and beneficiary of big government. Significant manufacturing in the state dates from
World War II when the federal government started pumping
huge sums into the California economy. (In recent times California has received nearly one-fifth of Department of Defense
spending and nearly half of NASA's budget.) The performance
of California news media in charting the depth of this relationship is a subject we explore later. Suffice it to say here that, as
far as most newspapers and broadcasting in the state go, corporate power is as invisible as the Hispanics.

California's agriculture is an extraordinarily diversified sector of economic activity concentrated into the narrowest of
ownership structures—the result of the nineteenth-century pat-

tern of land allocation and capital-intensive reclamation and irrigation work. The growers produce the goods—from winter lettuce to spring strawberries—at the cost of a high degree of labor exploitation. In the past, California media have taken the side of the growers. The *Bakersfield Californian,* for example, led the attack on the "Okies," the 1930s migrants from the Dust Bowl states who were discovered to be unwelcome intruders only after they ceased to depress wage levels downwards. Nowadays agriculture is often merely invisible: Merced in the valley is only 120 miles from San Francisco, but it could be in a different world if one judged by the coverage given agricultural affairs in the *San Francisco Chronicle.*

On the politics of water in the Central Valley depend many interests: not least the development and finance of agriculture in a premier farming state. Water is also the classic subject for single-issue lobbying in a state with a long tradition of this kind of political activity. Water often pits the interests of a wealthy few (especially big farmers) against the public interest, so is water constantly in the news? Occasional articles appear in the *Los Angeles Times;* the McClatchy *Bees* give solid reporting, and investigative/exposé water journalism is printed in *New West* magazine. But only a minority of California adults reads any one of these publications. Most urban and suburban daily newspapers largely ignore water reporting.

Admittedly water is complex. Take the $5 billion state scheme passed in 1980 which may one day carry water from the north to the south by means of a peripheral canal around the delta of the Sacramento River.

Water politics has not been made any simpler by the general skulduggery (ranging from sharp practice to open defiance of the law) which has accompanied it for decades of California history. The U.S. Reclamation Act of 1902 was designed to deliver water to arid and semi-arid regions of the west for the benefit of *small* farmers (originally defined as holding under 160 acres) who lived on their land. Various federal projects completed between 1940 and 1964 have provided huge quantities of cheap federal water that has been used by farms which are many times larger than the legal limit. Some of these farms are truly massive—for example, the J. G. Boswell farm at Cor-

coran is 60,000 acres of incredibly rich irrigated soil and is said to be the "world's largest cotton farm." Use of cheap federal water constitutes an enormous subsidy each year to such farms. California's agribusinesses have exerted pressure on vulnerable federal politicians—such as Senator Alan Cranston of California—and by 1980 they had largely been able to regularize the illegality. In other words, aggressive lobbying had eventually changed the federal law so as to make the water-grab legal.

Of course, the details of such a story are complex; but this would be true of any major political story about a big state's major industry. The *Los Angeles Times* historically has a bad record on water. Its publisher was the leader of the 1905–13 scheme which some people still call "the rape of the Owens Valley." The paper deliberately withheld news to the enormous personal financial gain of the publisher (through real estate purchases in advance of the news). Water may be too big a subject for news media which are intensely local. It remains necessary but often invisble.

The Visibility of Power

Most newspapers in the United States have at one time or another been intimate with the local owners of land and wielders of influence. As usual California just happens to provide some extreme examples. In Los Angeles for generations the interests of real estate were by definition those of the *Times*. And in San Jose's period as "the world's fastest growing city"—roughly 1950 to 1975—a similar conflation of interest occurred. Reporters used to see their editors at lunch with the local developer-seigneurs and get the message. Lou Cannon, a journalist with personal experience of the *Mercury* and *News* (the morning and evening San Jose papers now owned by the Knight-Ridder chain), describes the papers' "enthusiastic boosterism." Cannon notes: "The *Mercury-News*, interested in profits and circulation, formed a tight political alliance with the city government and specially with a public relations man turned city manager who was uncritically devoted to growth at any cost. . . ."[3] Oppo-

3. Lou Cannon, *Reporting: An Inside View*.

nents of land annexation were excluded from the papers while the City Hall beat became the most tightly controlled. The freeways were built, the land developed. "In the spirit of countinghouse newspapers everywhere," says Cannon, "the eyes of its owner were fixed firmly on the dollar signs of increased advertising and circulation growth. While the Valley of Heart's Delight was turned into a northern California replica of Los Angeles, the morning *Mercury* and its companion evening paper, the *News,* became two of the richest papers in the country."

Parallel accusations have been laid against media in the city of San Francisco. No pristine California countryside here, but a built-up city with large corporations and labor unions. Newspapers and television stations supported growth even when growth meant the destruction of the city's touristic skyline. The *Chronicle* and *Examiner* supplied supportive editorials about the large-scale downtown development called the Moscone Center (formerly the Yerba Buena Center). Why? Frederick M. Wirt,[4] a political scientist, believes that one reason must have been that both newspapers have headquarters adjoining the site; the *San Francisco Examiner* owned two additional adjoining lots. San Francisco radicals have long pointed to the 1000-foot-high transmitter built in the 1960s on Mount Sutro, an ugly structure which dominates the city, and is visible thirty miles away on a clear day. The result of a secret agreement between several stations, it symbolized "corporate television," said Bruce Brugmann, editor of the San Francisco *Bay Guardian,* a local radical newspaper. The tower is jointly owned by television stations KPIX (Westinghouse), KGO (ABC), and KRON (part of the *San Francisco Chronicle* interest).

Big Oil

Oil is big in California (as Table 5.2 shows). Two of the very largest companies, Standard Oil of California and Arco (Atlantic Richfield), are based in San Francisco and Los Angeles respectively. Several others—Getty, Occidental, and Union Oil— are Californian, too. Some date back to California's first great

4. Frederick M. Wirt, *Power in the City.*

oil boom in the 1890s, although it was in the early 1920s that
Los Angeles became the world's largest oil port and the related
oil refineries laid the basis for the famous smog problem of
later years. The state is still a major producer; the nodding
"donkey" pumps are a familiar sight across the south of the
state. California today is a well-situated base for the operations
of oil companies expanding into tar sands, oil shale, coal, and
other mining activities (such as copper and bauxite) in the western states and Alaska. For companies like Arco, with its intense
consciousness of media imagery, location at the hub of the entertainment industry is fitting.

Arco, whose 1979 revenues were $16.68 billion, is perhaps
the most environmentally controversial and the most sophisti-
cated at public relations of all the big oil companies. Its great
success has been in Alaskan oil and metals. But Arco sees itself
as an integrated natural resource company. More than almost
any other major oil company it is diversified not only into shale
oil and tar sands but into coal, copper, aluminum, uranium,
and other metals. In view of this diversification—which will
have a major environmental impact across several western
states—Arco has made and is making exceptional efforts to
build up a favorable image for the battles ahead. The company
specializes in a low-profile "use less gas" approach—even its gas
stations have a carefully quiet appearance. Its media involvement includes major contributions to public broadcasting; Arco
also owns the Aspen Institute of Humanistic Studies, the *Observer* newspaper of London, and *Harper's* magazine.

Getty is another oil company fascinated by the media. It has
an 85 percent share of a new network transmitting major
sports events across the country to cable television stations by
satellite. In 1980 it also signed up with four Hollywood majors—MCA, Columbia, Paramount, and Twentieth Century-
Fox—to distribute their products as a pay cable rival to Home
Box Office; this quickly ran into an anti-trust challenge.

Standard Oil of California has taken the chevron way to the
north of the state, to San Francisco. Its revenues for 1979 were
$30.94 billion. Much of its corporate PR is actually manufac-
tured in Los Angeles. "Of course," says John Yost, who handles
Standard's account with the J. Walter Thompson advertising

TABLE 5.2 Large Companies Headquartered in California 1979–1980 (Ten largest companies plus some entertainment/media companies)

Rank in California	Company	1979 Revenue (dollars)	Main Activities
1.	Standard Oil of California	30.94 billion	Oil
2.	Atlantic Richfield	16.68 billion	Oil
3.	Occidental Petroleum	9.55 billion	Oil
4.	Union Oil	7.98 billion	Oil
5.	Getty Oil	4.99 billion	Oil
6.	The Signal Cos.	4.24 billion	Engineering
7.	Litton Industries	4.09 billion	Electronics
8.	Lockheed	4.06 billion	Aerospace
9.	Foremost-McKesson	3.68 billion	Drugs
10.	Fluor Corp	3.54 billion	Engineering
19.	Times-Mirror	1.65 billion	Newspapers, TV stations
22.	MCA Inc.	1.27 billion	Film, TV production
33.	Walt Disney	797 million	Theme Parks
37.	Twentieth Century-Fox	678 million	Film production
56.	Metro-Goldwyn-Mayer	491 million	Hotel-Casinos
85.	Filmways	236 million	Books-Films
88.	Caesar's World	234 million	Casinos
	Bank		**Assets**
1.	Bank of America		106.27 billion

Source: *Los Angeles Times*, May 18, 1980.
Note: Figures relate to year ended December 1979 or before March 31, 1980.

agency in San Francisco: "Los Angeles is where the media skills are." But Yost says that the California audience is the toughest to convince of Big Oil's beneficence: "The hostility factor is very strong." Ever since the Sierra Club was founded in 1892, California has been a center for lobbying to protect the natural environment. In recent years nuclear power schemes have been the subject of several initiative propositions—with mixed results. But perhaps even more controversial in California have been the activities of the oil companies, especially as they affect the coast. The *Santa Barbara Press-News*, an otherwise undistinguished family-owned paper, earned a Pulitzer Prize for its work in apportioning the responsibility for a major 1969 oil leakage in the Santa Barbara Channel from a well owned by Union Oil.

In 1980 the California oil companies spent at least $8 million in defeating a proposition which would have placed an extra state tax on them. The advocates of the proposition made much, in their television advertisements, of "Pig Oil." But the oil companies fought back; and had the advantage of their regular propaganda services. Arco, for example, supplies to any television station a service of free video stories produced to a highly professional standard (and not looking at all like propaganda). In 1980 the service was costing Arco about $150,000 a year. Anthony Hatch, an experienced former WCBS television newsman, who launched the service in 1979, told us that the free video stories were taken (in April 1980) by 115 television and cable stations in the United States and by five foreign networks.

California Media and California Capitalism

Nowhere is the marriage of money, landownership, celebrity, and corporate interest better illustrated than in California's art world. The broad definition of art must be that which is collected by people with money. California's high and mighty love art and the kudos art brings with it. Their money circulates within a tight circle—as when, in 1973, Armand Hammer, head of Occidental Petroleum, paid over $5 million for the art collection of the late actor Edward G. Robinson. "Society" in southern California clusters around art—as the columns of *Los Angeles Times* society reporter Jody Jacobs show. Outside the Los Angeles County Museum of Art, which has a fine collection of painting and sculpture, there is a roster of founding benefactors. Here are the names on the plaque:

GENE AUTRY. Autry began in films as a singing cowboy with a famous horse, but progressed from one side of the camera to another. He is board chairman of Golden West Broadcasters, a substantial chain of radio outlets in California which also owns the key Los Angeles independent station, KTLA and has an interest in subscription television elsewhere in the United States.

MAX FACTOR. Factor was the celebrated make-up man who branched out from a career in the Hollywood studios to build up his own cosmetic business. "Now Mr. Max Factor of Hollywood," the commercial jingle used to run, "makes this promise to you. . . ."—it was a promise of youth, beauty and a passing resemblance to the stars.

NORMAN CHANDLER. The father of editor-in-chief Otis Chandler, Norman Chandler was publisher of the *Los Angeles Times* (1941–60). He made the early political career of Richard M. Nixon and in the 1940s and 1950s was responsible for the *Times*'s reputation as one of the most partisan Republican newspapers in the United States.

SAMUEL GOLDWYN. Goldwyn was for many years a major independent producer in Hollywood.

JAMES STEWART. Stewart is the movie actor who has specialized in Mr. Clean roles in such films as *Mr. Smith Goes to Washington* (1939) and *The Man Who Shot Liberty Valance* (1962).

HUGHES AIRCRAFT. The company was the plaything of Howard Hughes, man of many parts: he designed aircraft, made films, constructed Jane Russell's brassiere, and bought Las Vegas casinos.

BOB HOPE. Hope is the comedian, patriot, and walking advertisement for Palm Springs. He has recently become the advertising front man for California Federal Savings, one of the biggest savings and loan companies in the United States. In California, S & Ls took on a special prominence with the post-1945 construction boom.

CALIFORNIA FEDERAL SAVINGS AND LOAN (see above).

THE DISNEY FOUNDATION. The foundation is the charitable wing of Disney.

U.S. BORAX. This company, which is now owned by the British Rio Tinto Zinc, gave us Ronald Reagan: it used the former movie actor during the 1950s as the presenter of its television series *Death Valley Days*.

DOUGLAS AIRCRAFT. Along with Lockheed and Northrop, Douglas is one of the state's big aircraft makers. When Douglas's founder needed $15,000 during World War I to start building planes, to whom did he go? Harry Chandler, publisher of the *Los Angeles Times,* and father of Norman (above).

Three Corporate Californians—W. R. Hearst, A. P. Giannini, and W. E. Disney

The last name on the plaque outside the County Museum of Art is that of the W. R. Hearst Foundation, the philanthropic arm of the private corporation still bearing the name of the California media magnate. Hearst's name will recur in this book since he wielded his great power with such profligacy: as a newspaper owner, a would-be politician, and later a political king-maker, as builder of a pleasure dome to rival Kublai Khan, as a movie producer and impresario, and as a truly Californian myth-maker.

But if Hearst was the wielder of untold private power, he was also a peculiar capitalist. His fortune was derived from his father, U.S. Senator George Hearst, and his father's success in acquiring claims to precious metals in the hills of California and Nevada as well as in Montana, South Dakota, and Mexico. Hearst senior left his wife and only son a fortune based on gold, silver, and copper mines scattered from Montana to Mexico. Almost childlike in his thirst for acquisitions, Hearst junior was never an investor in the classic capitalist sense. As a young man he was given the *San Francisco Examiner* by his father, who had bought it as a prop to his political amibitons. W. R. Hearst's spending on it and on the other papers, and magazines—and later film studies, radio stations, and newsreels—was never cumulative or sequential.

Fortune magazine provided a marvelous description of Hearst-the-capitalist in a long article published in 1935. The core of Hearst's empire, said *Fortune,* is accumulation. "A few hundred years ago when kings and princes lived upon the land and got money from who-knew-where, this sort of thing was common. . . . The fact is that Mr. Hearst has made his money off the bourgeois world but he has treated it as if it came to him by divine right rather than by his own shrewdness. In a word Mr. Hearst is an economic anchronism."

He was, as *Fortune* went on to describe, an anachronism with a $250 million fortune. The empire took in great tracts of Californian land: his Xanadu at San Simeon on the coast above San Luis Obispo, his German-style village at Wyntoon in the north of the state; downtown San Francisco and Los Angeles had swathes of Hearst-owned land. It was best known through the broad chain of Hearst newspapers published coast to coast in almost every major American city. Hearst's Cosmopolitan Pictures ate millions of dollars of Hearst money, first as an independent production company in New York; later linked with the Metro-Goldwyn-Mayer operations in Hollywood, and later still with Warner Brothers. Cosmopolitan Pictures was never a great production company. Romantics like to think Hearst's interest in films stemmed in large measure from his love for actress Marion Davies. Louis B. Mayer of MGM could live with Cosmpolitan's flops, he often said, as long as the great Hearst publicity machine kept rolling for MGM's pictures. In addition to Cosmpolitan Pictures, Hearst owned half of Hearst-Metrotone News, one of American's biggest newsreel operations until the thirties. MGM owned the other half. Its greatest asset was MGM's theatrical distribution and exhibition. In the heyday of his fortunes, Hearst had the run of the Californian airwaves, too. He began buying radio stations in 1928 with the ambition of owning a station in every city where he had a newspaper. By 1935 the eight stations he owned included KYA San Francisco, KELW Burbank, and KEME Santa Monica.

But Hearst must in the last analysis be seen as a premodern; his empire was never consolidated to stand the test of time. The revenues of the Hearst Corporation in 1978 were $500 million—a big drop compared with assets of $250 million at 1935 prices. There is an interesting comparison to be made with one of Hearst's greatest contemporaries, a fellow California innovator. This was Amadeo Peter Giannini, the San Jose-born banker who created the Bank of Italy, later the Bank of America, the first great American branch bank, the creator of consumer credit. Unlike Hearst, Giannini was a self-made man; unlike Hearst he left a sound corporation behind him and his son. Giannini was an independent Californian capitalist who took on the East—meaning Wall Street—and lost his freedom. Hearst, too, left San Francisco to pursue politics from a New York City base—but retired from the contest. Giannini created the Transamerica Corporation in the 1920s to be his instrument for a national branch-banking system (which required a change in the law). But in Washington both men failed. The F.D.R. administration pursued Giannini; after World War II the anti-trust laws required the separation of the Bank of America from Transamerica, which had developed from strictly a financial holding company into the general purpose conglomerate it is today. Transamerica built the pyramid-pointed skyscraper that is such a distinctive feature of downtown San Francisco. Transamerica (which has now moved to New York) owns a Hollywood major (United Artists), Budget Rent-a-Car, and Occidental Life Insurance. In a sense, too, New York won out over California capitalism as represented by W. R. Hearst. The reorganization of his ramshackle empire was carried out during the 1930s by the Crocker National Bank of San Francisco, and to this day the Hearst Corporation remains a private company. But as power slipped from W.R. to his sons and their executives, so power shifted eastward. The Hearst Corporation's diversified magazine, syndication, and television interests are still held back by the troubled newspapers.

Comparison might be made with a third Californian innovator, slightly younger than Giannini and Hearst, and ultimately the most successful. He is Walter Elias Disney. Raised in Kansas City, Disney migrated to California aged twenty-one. Local business in the shape of bankers was none too kind to his vision of nationally distributed cinema cartoons—Richard Schickel points out how bankers are often portrayed in the original Disney animated features as evil figures. But the evolution of plain Walt Disney into corporate Walt Disney Productions was eventually a great feat of California capitalist enterprise—the advent of eastern money in the shape of the American Broadcasting Company in the fifties was short lived. Walt Disney concluded a deal with ABC (and hence with Paramount Theaters) by which he got capital for Disneyland, but by 1961 Walt Disney Productions had bought out ABC. Interestingly, Hearst had a useful walk-on part in Disney's success. Back in 1931, mammoth King Features, part of the Hearst empire, came forward with an offer to syndicate Disney's cartoon strip.

Economic historians have ascribed to California three phases of development. First, an extractive era during the nineteenth century when California's precious metals financed economic development not only throughout the rest of the United States but the rest of the world. Next there was a period when agriculture was the state's leading activity. This was also the age of the Bank of Italy, when Giannini's enthusiasm for branch banking allowed capital to be shifted from the coastal towns to the agricultural interior of the state and back again in a remarkable effort of self-financing of capital-intensive cultivation. Contemporaries were so impressed by the scale of the bank's involvement in financing farm mortgages and underwriting the seasonal crops of the San Joaquin Valley that they exaggerated its scale. In 1939 some 3.6 percent of the arable land of the state was in mortgages held by the Bank of America. Not only agriculture was the Bank of America's province: Giannini had an early role in film finance and in the industries stimulated by the growth of Los Angeles, among them the garment trade. The young movie industry raised much of its capital locally. As early as 1918 the Bank of Italy was lending $50,000 to the Famous-Players Lasky Company. With remarkable prescience (for a banker) Giannini realized how star potential reduced the risk of films. A. P. Giannini's brother, then in charge of the Los Angeles end of the Bank of Italy, once said: "If a film is offered to me starring Doug (Fairbanks), Charlie (Chaplin), Harold (Lloyd) or any of half a dozen leading actors it is as good as cash." Thus California agriculture had a place in the financial history of film; and Mary Pickford was not only America's sweetheart, she was also the Bank of America's sweetheart.

The Californian Media Also Like Big Government

The third phase in Californian economic development is dated by most historians from World War II. During the conflict the state's economy acquired a recognizably modern form—by acquiring manufacturing industry. The war meant federal dollars; the postwar success of Californian capitalism has depended as much on Washington, D.C., as on Wall Street. Big government meant defense contracts for the aircraft and later the aerospace industry; it meant research and development funds for Silicon Valley outside San Jose. By 1979 the United States was spending $53 billion a year in the state—mostly in social security and defense. Of that, some $18.5 billion came from the Pentagon.

Here are two quick examples of the government connection. Walt Disney, no friend in his politics to large-scale governmental spending, benefited from Uncle Sam during WW II: his studio designed over 1100 insignias for various military outfits and was well paid for the job. Another example came from the J. Walter Thompson office in San Francisco where we spoke to an executive. A large part of its billings come from Standard Oil of California, so the reception area was understandably bedecked with the blue and red chevrons of Standard's corporate logo. But alongside the chevrons were stripes of another kind. Another of JWT's very big accounts is the United States Marine Corps: the stripes belonged to a recruiting sergeant displayed on posters throughout the office. Marines are big in California. Marine camps and bases follow in rapid succession from Orange County south to San Diego, and the Marine Corps' Camp Pendleton, with its 18 miles of beach, is ironically the last hope of people who want to prevent San Diego's merging into greater Los Angeles. The Marines have always been the service spiritually closest to Hollywood, and some of the Marines' greatest cinematic triumphs have been filmed on the beaches and hills of Camp Pendleton.

The Secret Life of the Media Business

The following sounds like an underground publication trying to out-do Hollywood in melodrama:

> To his associates in Los Angeles, Sidney R. Korshak is a highly successful labor lawyer, an astute business adviser to major corporations, a multi-millionaire with immense influence and many connections, a friend of top Hollywood stars and executives.
> He is so entrenched in Hollywood's social and business structures that he mingles easily with such enter-

tainers as Dinah Shore, Debbie Reynolds, and Tony Martin and with such prestigious businessmen as Charles G. Bludhorn, Chairman of Gulf and Western Industries, and Lew Wasserman, chief executive of MCA Inc, the entertainment conglomerate.
But Sidney Korshak leads a double life.
To scores of Federal, state and local law enforcement officials, Mr. Korshak is the most important link between organized crime and legitimate business. They describe him as a behind-the-scenes "fixer" who has been instrumental in helping criminal elements gain power in union affairs and infiltrate the leisure and entertainment industries.

But this was no underground publication. This was the start of a four-part series of articles in the *New York Times* (June 27–30, 1976) by investigative reporter Seymour M. Hersh.

The articles—based on 300 interviews—went into enormous detail. Among the details which were embarrassing to Los Angeles business in general and Hollywood in particular were the following:

—Korshak controlled Associated Booking Corporation, the third largest theatrical booking agency.

—His Hollywood friends included Robert Evans, producer of *The Godfather.*

—"Sidney Korshak is probably the most important man socially out here," said Joyce Haber, the Hollywood columnist. "If you're not invited to his Christmas party, it's a disaster."

—Lew Wasserman was quoted as calling Korshak "a very good personal friend" and one of he forty or fifty people in Hollywood with influence.

—Sidney Korshak was born in Chicago in 1907, the son of a Jewish immigrant from Lithuania. He attended the University of Wisconsin, qualified as a lawyer, and then started to defend members of the Capone gang.

—One of his criminal contacts was Willie Bioff (who was a mobster union official in Hollywood for IATSE).

—Korshak after 1945 became an important man in Chicago. He specialized in smoothing down labor problems. He also gave frequent parties for Chicago businessmen, where they could meet "showgirls" or, in the words of one judge, "girls costing $250 or more."

—Later Korshak moved into apparently legitimate activities specializing as a labor lawyer and strike fixer.

—In 1950 he blackmailed Senator Estes Kefauver.

—Korshak acquired a house in Hollywood. He was involved in various activities in Las Vegas in conjunction with the Teamsters.

—In 1962 Korshak settled a Teamster strike (by parking lot attendants) which threatened to delay the opening of the new Dodgers stadium in Los Angeles.

—In the late 1960s and early 1970s—while still known to the FBI and other federal agencies as a hoodlum lawyer—Korshak was involved in many high level deals in Los Angeles, apparently in a completely legitimate capacity. One such deal involved MGM, MCA, Gulf and Western, and $75 million.

Lew Wasserman is quoted in the *New York Times* articles on Korshak's criminal dealings: "I don't believe them. I've never seen him with so-called syndicate members or organization members." But the articles make it quite clear that Korshak did not behave like a typical lawyer—instead some of his personal behavior was a caricature of routines favored by Hollywood's screen mobster lawyers. Korshak apparently attended complex meetings without any papers and kept no records. He made phone calls from public telephones, although he would use regular telephones in an expensive restaurant which he himself partly owned . . . and so on. Based on the *New York Times* accounts, nobody who had been to a meeting with this man could have doubted that he was a very unusual lawyer indeed. The only possible conclusion is that Hollywood and other California businessmen turned a blind eye on Korshak's Mafia connections because he was such an efficient Mr. Fix-It, especially with nagging labor problems.

The second scandal concerns David Begelman, who was found guilty of misappropriating $61,008 in corporate funds and $23,000 in expenses while he was president of Columbia

Pictures. Jack Valenti—the movie industry's national spokesman—dismissed the stealing of a paltry $84,000 as something which, if it had happened in the cement industry, would have caused no interest. The judge who heard the case seemed to agree; Begelman incurred a small fine, was put on probation, and sentenced to make a film—on the evils of drugs—which he did to the judge's (and others') satisfaction. Soon Begelman was partially reinstated at Columbia by being given a $1.5 million contract as an independent producer. After various other events—including the sacking of Begelman's own boss, Alan Hirschfield—Begelman was put in charge of the reactivated film studio at MGM.

Several aspects of this affair were disturbing. One was the way in which the facts came to light. One of Begelman's phony checks had been made out to the well-known actor Cliff Robertson—and Robertson seems to have been one of the very few people in Hollywood who would not have agreed to Begelman's plea to hush the whole thing up. Robertson was unusual in several ways: the only star who was also a board member at the Screen Actors' Guild; an independently wealthy man in addition to his acting income; and a political activist with friends in Washington, including the publisher of the *Washington Post*.

That is another worrying aspect. The whole thing came out only in the *Washington Post* after Robertson had failed to interest the Los Angeles press in skulduggery by a highly placed Hollywood person. The way in which the story emerged and the speed with which it was subsequently settled left a nasty suspicion that there was more here than met the eye. Perhaps there was not, but the impression created was that at the top levels of the industry a $84,000 robbery was very little.

Together these stories present an unsavory picture of Hollywood and an unflattering picture of how the local media cover a local industry. A small group of senior people know each other and regard themselves as above the law, or at least believe—to use Jack Valenti's favored example—that behavior which might get by in the cement industry should also be good enough for Hollywood. Both Korshak and Begelman were deal-makers; Korshak was a specialist in labor deals, while Begelman was a former agent, a very successful film-making executive at Columbia, and thus a man with the golden touch in making film deals.

Most of all these two stories suggest that the entertainment industry is good not only at publicizing itself but also usually very successful at keeping invisible that which it wishes to hide.

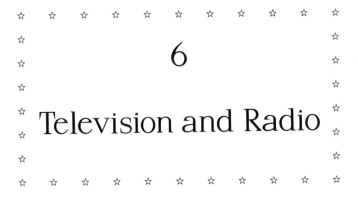

6

Television and Radio

In the history of the American media, questions of rights under The First Amendment have been most important. Freedom of the press and of broadcasters to gather information has more often been the issue than has the quality of information or its volume. Liberal-minded writers on the media have concentrated on questions of access to information—different altogether from information's adequacy. There is still only a sketchy framework for discussing the motivation of television stations or newspapers to gather the "truth," even if there were no appreciable barriers to its discovery. How they present the "truth" once gathered is another matter. In Chapter 5 we argued that important sections of California life—its agriculture, its ethnic relations, even its own media industries—appeared often to be left in darkness, out of the media's spotlight. If California is typical, there is a great and worrying gap in the supply of intra-state news in the United States. The reputation of television coverage of state-wide politics in California is not bright. The general judgment of Ron Powers[1] seems especially true of California: "Somewhere between Washington and other

1. Ron Powers, *The Newscasters,* p. 67.

capitals (the television networks' territories) and City Hall (theoretically the purview of the local station) exists an invisible realm of political and corporate power, decision-making and policy-setting, economic theorizing and personal ethics that does not get monitored on a day-to-day basis by television news."

Powers has provided a definition of "disinformation," the news you do not get. Disinformation is not a problem of television alone. The *San Francisco Examiner's* bureau chief in Sacramento gave us his working estimate of it. "D.G.S.N.R.," he said. Comprehension briefly failed us. "Dull Government Shit Nobody Reads." He elaborated: what he meant was the legislative work of the California assembly and senate in Sacramento and the activities of the state's 280,000 or so employees. Inadequate coverage of government in California (as opposed to the personalities in that government such as the governor) is widely perceived as a problem. Rollin Post, a Bay Area news executive of considerable experience who has worked for such television stations as KQED and KPIX, put the matter this way. The sins of commission in the relationship of media and politics are well attested: look at the career of William Randolph Hearst, he said. But the sins of omission—the absence of television coverage of essential events and processes—are probably more important nowadays, and yet harder to criticize since it means probing the economics of media production.

Economics were behind the withdrawal during the early and mid-1970s of nearly every one of the major California television stations from permanent coverage of Sacramento. The major stations had installed camera crews in the state capital during the 1960s. But one by one the crews were pulled out by news managers in the throes of the "big news," "news-as-entertainment," "happy talk news" revolution—California's role in which we will discuss below.

Television coverage of politics in the state was at such a low ebb that the extraordinary circumstances of the 1974 gubernatorial election were made possible. Mary Ellen Leary has made an influential study of the race:[2] insofar as the electorate relied

2. Mary Ellen Leary, *Phantom Politics.*

on television for their news of issues and campaigning in the fight for the governorship of the great state of California, it was left in utter ignorance. Leary found that broadcast news reports on the six major San Francisco and Los Angeles television stations over the final two months of the election campaign were so sparse that the election received only 2.3 percent of total television news time. When the share of that coverage provided by KNBC, the Los Angeles station owned and operated by NBC, is omitted, the five other major stations gave only 1.5 percent of their total news time to the election, and much of that was spent on superficial reports one minute or less in duration. KNBC had one-third of the coverage of the six major stations and, Leary says, "was the only effort in Californian broadcast media to report the race as a continuing event."

Lack of coverage suited one of the contenders, Jerry Brown, very well. He had a famous name; his father had been a popular state governor between 1958 and 1966. A dull, secretive campaign in which his name alone got over to voters was what he wanted; even a minority poll would suit (as it turned out California had in November 1974 the smallest ratio of people participating in a state contest of all the American states). Without precedent, Brown and his Republican opponent agreed to a pact regulating when and where they would be available for the media—meaning television; the hauteur of print journalists prevented their agreeing to any such scheme. It was a bad mistake by the Republican, Houston Flournoy. What ensued was a carefully stage-managed contest, largely invisible to the electorate. More important things were happening locally. Leary quotes a television news director in San Diego: "I haven't seen any candidates for office do or say anything worth putting on the air—not when I have big stories on cab drivers being arrested for transporting illegal aliens, drug busts . . . large buildings being burned down in major blazes. . . ."[3]

Leary's book was influential: we interviewed few news executives in television, radio, or newspapers who were not keenly aware of the book and the issues it raised. Perhaps be-

3. Ibid., p. 47.

cause of her, coverage of the gubernatorial race four years later was clearly stronger. Even station KRON-TV in San Francisco, which had largely ignored the 1974 race, dispatched two cameras crews to travel round the state with contenders Jerry Brown and Evelle Younger. Yet day-to-day coverage of Sacramento continues to be scanty, to judge from our own ten months' monitoring of television news in the two metropolitan areas. Southern California's 14 million people were served with Sacramento political news by one man—Doug Kriegel of KNBC-TV. If, as Ed Salzman of the *California Journal* told us, people in Los Angeles don't know where Sacramento is, and do not care, then television is partly responsible.

The Sights of California

"Happy talk" news was an American television phenomenon of the 1970s. The original formulas for presenting the news in a more "entertaining" fashion did not originate in California— but there are few other places where they have been applied with such intensity and rigor as in the major California media markets. The formulas of, say, the news consultancy firm of Frank N. Magid Associates specify various formats, such as dual presenters, the necessity of a certified meteorologist, "team atmosphere through conversation in interchange."[4] In other words, the news becomes happier and snappier: the broadcasts are broken up into segments containing short items heavily illustrated by film and videotape; the show revolves around an anchor and co-presenters who read the news with panache and dress according to a set of ground rules. Most important, the news should include as little national or international content as possible unless stories from outside the locality are so major that they affect the lives of the television audience directly. This emerges in California as a fairly sensationalist package of stories, reminiscent of a popular mass circulation British daily newspaper. Here are two typical half-hours from the leading San Francisco and Los Angeles stations. The obvious characteristics are action, pace, an almost dizzy attempt to keep the audience from getting bored.

4. Marvin Barrett (ed.), *Moments of Truth.*

Local news is important for commercial reasons. Such local programing carries about 14 minutes per hour of advertising; it earns a station recognition; scores points with the Federal Communications Commission; hooks the audience for the evening programing after 8 p.m. KABC in Los Angeles was typical in 1979 in running two hours of local news from 5 to 7 p.m. followed by a half-hour of network news. There was also a half-hour of local news after prime time at 11–11:30 p.m. Then the CBS station added an extra half-hour of local news, and in 1980 KABC added a full hour—resulting in three hours of local news on KABC at 4–7 p.m. But volume of news is no guarantee of quality.

News has probably been made more sensational and more entertaining in California because of the intense competition that obtains in the Los Angeles and San Francisco news markets. Los Angeles has twelve commercial television stations within its "area of dominant influence." They are immensely profitable. For example, the Los Angeles commercial television stations together in 1978 generated profits of $64.8 million. Los Angeles's three network owned-and-operated stations have to compete with four major (VHF) independent stations as well as five other commercial stations: Los Angeles local news has to be entertaining partly because there are so many points on the dial where viewers can switch from local news to "pure" entertainment in the shape of the re-runs and game shows being offered as counter-programing on the independents. The Bay Area market is smaller: but the competition between ABC's owned-and-operated station (KGO) and local affiliates of the two other networks is fierce.

Because of this competition, both areas have bought the skills of the news consultants and news fixers in prodigious quantities. The "talent," the news presenters, switch stations at bewildering speed; station formats chop and change, except when, in the case of the ABC stations, the format brings success in the ratings. In both areas, in the early days of local television news the CBS affiliates (KNXT and KPIX) were far ahead. By the mid 1970s the ABC stations had taken the lead. KGO in San Francisco built its rise around success at 11 p.m. Its then news director Pat Polillo told us that when he arrived in the Bay Area in 1970 from the East people switched off at 11. But

TABLE 6.1 ABC Owned-and-Operated News in Los Angeles
25 Minutes of KABC News: Tuesday, February 13, 1979

6.00	EYEWITNESS NEWS. . . .No. 1 in Southern California . . . Quick headlines	
6.00½	Deaths follow L.A. showing of violent movie?	Clips, Film* & Interview
6.02	Verdict in murder case, L.A.	Film & Int.
6.04	Police-files shredding, L.A.	Film & Int.
6.05	Rifkind accused of 2nd electronic fraud, local	Film
6.06	World Wide Church of God accosts public, LAX airport	Film & Int.
6.07	First of two-part series on WWCofG's money. Members of church questioned	Film & Int.
6.11	Robbery of antique violas. Unusual crime. Suspects apprehended. Anchor's comment: "Well caught cops."	Film & Int.
6.12	COMMERCIALS and *Hollywood Squares* promotion	2 mins.
6.14	Fire on Sunset Boulevard	Film only
6.15	Ship, volatile gas, L.A. harbor	Film only
6.16	Earthslide, Laguna Beach. Expensive homes destroyed	Film & Int.
6.17	L.A. flood control district winding up cashless	Film only
6.19	COMMERCIALS	2 mins.
6.00½	Deaths follow L.A. showing of violent movie?	Film only Studio & Film
6.02	Verdict in murder case, L.A.	
6.26	Weather ends.	

*Film in the generic sense; mainly in fact videotape.

by building on personalities and working hard on the news content, Polillo says, he made KGO number one. The ABC affiliates seized the formula: they went for sensation and a new brand of "coping" journalism. KABC ran, for example, in 1975 a mini-documentary series on breast cancer and how to cope, eliciting a great amount of local interest. It also, in 1976, spent $1.4 million on advertising the names, faces, and personalities of its news anchor team. KABC's and KGO's success has caused a succession of adjustments in the staff and formats of their

TABLE 6.2   ABC Owned-and-Operated News in San Francisco
25 Minutes of KGO News: Friday, March 2, 1979

6.00	Promos "News Scene": Promises porno, People's Temple and prostitution stories. Exclusive on foreign students swindle, cancer	
	COMMERCIALS	
6.02	People's Temple assets being liquidated	Film & Int.
	Anchor winds up item	
6.04	Vice in S.F.—Homosexual angle	
6.05	More vice—S.F. sex shows	Film
6.05½	Murder in San Mateo	Film
6.07	East Bay arrest of congressman's son for murder attempt	Film
	Senator's son on murder charge	
6.10	Crime story	Film
6.10½	Local suicide	
6.11	Santa Clara fire	Film & Int.
	Anchor: "coming up next"	
6.13	COMMERCIALS	2 mins.
6.15	Towing service in S.F.	Film
	Gasoline crisis	Film & Int.
6.16	BART Tunnel story	
	Novelty item: San Mateo Traveling Hotel	Film & Int.
	Chat about this between anchors	
6.21	COMMERCIALS	2 mins.
6.23	Nuclear weapons at U.C. Berkeley (stresses "one of the world's greatest universities")	Film
	Novelty item about end of frozen meat imports	Film
6.25	Foreign students in local schools	Film & Int.

rivals, especially the third running KNBC in Los Angeles and the NBC affiliate KRON in the Bay Area. In San Diego, too, the ABC affiliate had the top news show from 5 p.m. to 6 p.m. and after 11 in 1979. The station manager confirmed to us that the most highly paid talents on the station were the leading male and female anchors and the weatherperson—all earning in 1979 around $100,000, several times more than members of the reporting staff.

California news programing in its four major markets—San Francisco (fifth in scale nationally), Los Angeles (second after New York), San Diego (1.5 million), and Sacramento-Stockton—has a number of attributes in common. One is the star quality of the "talent," the "bench" of anchors who present the news: they are the newest stars to join the pantheon of media celebrity in America. Marty Levin, anchor at KGTV (ABC affiliate) in San Diego, told us that people were always asking him for his autograph—which nobody had done when he did the same job in Seattle. "Being near to Los Angeles seems to make people want to hero worship," he mused. Maybe; but there is no doubt that both the San Diego and San Francisco news markets act as feeders of talent to Los Angeles, which itself swaps and supplies anchors with and to Chicago and New York. At the head of the line-up on Los Angeles's most successful station, KABC, was a veritable regional star, Jerry Dunphy. Recruited from KNXT TV in 1975, Dunphy is silver-haired and behaves as what is he is, the doyen of a strange breed who are half-journalist and half-show-business entertainer. Dunphy's status is not harmed by the fact that his son-in-law is the lieutenant-governor of the state, Mike Curb. His counterpart in the Bay Area is a younger man, a former baseball player, Van Amberg (born Fred Van Amberg). An engaging personality, Amberg told us he takes "average guy positions as most issues"; determined to keep the news peppy and exciting, he wants always to show the "people side" of breaking news, be it the Hearst affair or the Zodiac killings.

Such anchors never stand alone. Their success, according to the Magid formulas, relies on their participation in a team. Dunphy shared the six o'clock slot in 1979–80 with blond Christine Lund; Amberg shared with a staid older man, Jerry Jensen, and brunette Marcia Brandwynne (who took flight to greater fortune in Los Angeles during 1980). Each team had a range of other members—many, like Amberg, recruits from such areas of celebrity as sports. The team, by Magid decree, must contain a weatherperson. Few weather people in America compare with the personality recruited by KABC, Dr. George Fischbeck.

Californians love their weather forecasts, and they especially like their forecasters to point in mock sorrow to the bad weather back east while California basks in sun. Dr. George, bow-tied, schoolmasterly, and ebulliently eccentric, windmills into action to supply this need for as long as four or five minutes at a time. He enthuses and hurrahs; gets lost in the detail of his—admittedly excellent—charts; sometimes he even forgets to sum up the next day's weather. But the play's the thing.

Action is the common denominator of the successful news shows. KABC, like its competitors and counterparts, uses actuality material in prodigal quantities. In 1979 it had 14 mini-cameras in action, producing original video material from the Los Angeles area. All the stations rejoice in high technology: one San Francisco station can, by means of its "instacams" and related transmission apparatus, get a picture live on the air from any point from the Oregon border to Monterey. The stations have taken to the air in another sense. In the Bay Area, KRON and KPIX have helicopters leased on a long-term basis for their exclusive use; KGO regularly rents one.

A source of much action film, the helicopters, transmuted into "Telecopter 4" for KRON and "Skyscene 7" for KGO, are good public relations. They may also give a competitive edge. According to Polillo, "If you knew a very major event was going on in San Francisco and the Bay Area and you turned on the television and two of the television stations are telling you about it, while the third station is showing it to you, I think there's no question about which one you would watch."[5] Coverage of politics could never be as exciting.

. . . And Sounds

Radio is ubiquitous in California in a way matched in few other areas. In Los Angeles, for example, there are 5.7 radios per household, excluding car radios, far above the national average. The state's climate means that much leisure is taken out of doors, but within earshot of radio. Southern California's mobility involves a lot of people spending a lot of time cooped up in automobiles with little to do but listen to radio: 87 percent of all journeys to work in Los Angeles and Orange counties are

5. Quoted in *Feed/back*, Fall 1979, p. 11.

by car. All in all, some four out of five adults in the two-county area listen to radio every day, making the area comparatively profitable for stations able to persuade their advertisers they will reach more than a severely fractionalized segment of the total population. Many do. The revenues of Los Angeles County radio stations in 1977 overtook New York's; in 1979 they topped $105 million. Los Angeles, in particular, is a radio area since, in the self-serving words of Bob Light, president of the Southern California Broadcasters Association, you add to "radio's natural attributes of economy, selectivity, mobility, immediacy, flexibility the special regional characteristics of climate, size, mobility and life style."

California at large is probably in the vanguard as far as its radio goes. The sheer scale of radio production—eighty plus stations in Los Angeles, sixty in the Bay Area—makes apparent the problem of fragmentation. California is radio Babel. The Federal Communications Commission's proposals to reduce the signal strength of some stations and to allow many thousands more on the air suggest that Los Angeles' density of radio coverage may provide a vision of the future. It is by no means an unhappy vision, though it may not make many people's fortunes. In the big media stakes, radio is a puny infant. The total annual advertising revenue of all Los Angeles radio stations is less than half that of one newspaper, the *Los Angeles Times*.

California's two major urban areas are both well served by their all-news stations. All news is a format with some claim to origins on the West Coast, both in Portland, Oregon, and across the Mexican border at Tijuana, where in the 1950s an embryonic service consisting of reading the AP and UPI tapes was developed at station XTRA for the San Diego market. The all-news station in the Bay Area is KCBS-AM; it was, said Martin Thompson, AP's bureau chief in San Francisco, a vital source of spot news on which AP depended for tips. KCBS and its counterpart in Los Angeles, KNX (both owned and operated by CBS radio), are profitable because they cull an up-market group for advertisers: men over thirty-five. Like California television, however, the all-news stations have a strict definition of "local"—all else comes from the CBS network. Peter McCoy, general manager of KCBS said: "Local is things of direct or personal concern; while oil cartel decisions may influence the audience, they are much more concerned about the weather and what their sports team did last night." KNX station manager George Nicholauw told us that this station had 50 on-air journalists and 93 news personnel. The station combines strong doses of politics with a frenetic pace, rapidly alternating anchor voices, and the inevitable weather, traffic, and sport. KNX's main competition comes from the Group W station KFWB, which organizes its newscasts in half-hour blocks to coincide with the flow of commuting traffic. Even in the daytime hours between morning and afternoon drivetime there are still, on average, 1,122,000 cars at any one time on the freeways and roads of Los Angeles and Orange counties. Los Angeles radio also offers an all-talk station, KABC, which specializes in headline news, features, some serious daytime interviews with prominent people, and massive quantities of sportstalk.

Los Angeles is rich in music radio, and some current trends provide an insight into nationwide trends (see Table 6.3). One is the apparent decline of "Top 40" radio. Station KHJ used to be one of the most important stations for "breaking out" a record. In 1965 it hired the innovating radio producer Bill Drake who devised the so-called Boss Radio format of a very limited playlist of currently popular singles. The theory was that, the less likely the listeners were to hear something they did not like, the less likely they were to switch to a competing station. Drake later founded the successful Los Angeles-based syndication company Drake Chenault, one of the biggest specialist radio programers in the country. In 1979 Radio Arts International of Burbank, for example, programmed some 110 stations across the country with one of three formats: adult middle of the road, adult contemporary, and "bright and easy" country. In the later 1970s KHJ declined, making a succession of changes, as the old tried and trusted formula of the Top 40 both with and without personality disc jockeys failed to boost the ratings.

AM radio in Los Angeles is now second string to FM. According to Arbitron figures, 52 percent of the available LA radio audience by 1980 listened to an FM station. James Brown,[6]

6. James Brown, "Los Angeles Radio: Earful of Contradictions," *Advertising Age*, May 21 1979.

radio columnist for the *Los Angeles Times,* attributes the decline of AM stations to their inability to hold not only younger audiences now attracted by the less commercial FM stations playing whole albums but also the older audience seeking middle of the road music and finding it on such prosperous FM stations as KBIG and KJOI ("beautiful music").

Alternative Sights and Sounds

The bizarre strain in California life is not absent even from its radio. The showbusiness-inclined evangelist of the 1920s Aimee Semple McPherson ran, from the top of her Angelus Temple, a radio station which played a pioneer role in the subsequently extensive religious broadcasting in Los Angeles. The station wandered all over the wave band until, after repeated warnings, the federal government intervened. The Secretary of Commerce (President-to-be Herbert Hoover) thereupon received the following telegram from the irate evangelist: "Please order your minions of State to leave my station alone. You cannot expect the Almighty to abide by your wavelength nonsense. When I offer my prayers to him I must fit into his wave reception. Open this station at once."[7]

In California's Central Valley at Delano, between five and seven most afternoons can be heard the voice of a man who died several years ago. His widow runs station KCHJ and programs that time slot with old tapes of the dead disc jockey doing his "starduster" routine with sounds from the Big Band era.

The most influential of California sounds is less exotic. Station KSAN FM in San Francisco was a genuine attempt, in its very early days, to be an "alternative." KSAN's album-based progressive musical format is probably the best known of the relics of 1960s San Francisco radicalism; but like most residues of the 1960s it evolved fairly steadily into a pillar of the seventies' establishment. In the 1980s it has gone country.

KSAN was the child of a California radio innovator of the same order as Bill Drake—Tom Donahue. On the San Fran-

7. Quoted in Sydney Head, *Broadcasting in America,* Boston, 1976 ed.

TABLE 6.3 Los Angeles County and Orange County Radio Stations, 1979

Station-AM	Frequency (kilohertz)	Format
KABC	790	Talk
KALI	1430	Spanish
KAVL	610	Middle-of-the-Road/Top 40
KBRT	740	Inspirational/Contemporary
KDAY	1580	Black
KEZY	1190	Album-Oriented Rock
KFAC	1330	Classical
KFI	640	Contemporary
KFRN	1280	Religious
KFWB	980	News
KGER	1390	Religious/Inspirational
KGIL	1260	Adult Contemporary
KGRB	900	Nostalgic/Big Band
KHJ	930	Contemporary/Top 40
KIEV	870	Talk/Religious
KIIS	1150	Adult Contemporary
KKTT	1230	Black Contemporary
KKZZ	1380	News/Talk
KLAC	570	Country & Western
KLIT	1220	Religious
KMPC	710	Adult Contemporary
KNX	1070	News
KPOL	1540	Middle-of-the-Road
KPPC	1240	Inspirational/Ethnic
KRLA	1110	Top 40/Oldies/Disco
KROQ	1500	Album-Oriented Rock
KTNQ	1020	Top 40
KTYM	1460	Talk/Religious/Language
KUXX	1470	Adult Contemporary
KWIZ	1480	Adult Contemporary
KWKW	1300	Spanish
KWOW	1600	Oldies

Station-FM	Frequency (megahertz)	Format
KACE	103.9	Contemporary/Soul
KBIG	104.3	Beautiful Music
KBOB	98.3	Nostalgic/Big Band
KBPK*	90.1	Educational
KCRW*	89.9	Educational
KCSN*	88.5	Educational
KEZY	95.9	Album-Oriented Rock
KFAC	92.3	Classical

Station-FM (cont.)	Frequency (kilohertz)	Format
KABC	790	Talk
KFSG	96.3	Gospel Music
KGIL	94.3	Adult Contemporary
KHOF	99.5	Religious
KHTZ	97.1	Gentle Country
KIIS	102.7	Disco
KIQQ	100.3	Ablum-Oriented Rock
KJI H	102.3	Black Contemporary
KJOI	98.7	Beautiul Music
KKGO	105.1	Jazz
KLON*	88.1	Educational
KLOS	95.5	Album-Oriented Rock
KLVE	107.5	Spanish
KMAX	107.1	Inspirational/Ethnic
KMET	94.7	Album-Oriented Rock
KNAC	105.5	Progressive Rock
KNHS*	89.7	Educational
KNOB	97.9	Beautiful Music
KNX	93.1	Adult Contemporary
KOCM	103.1	Middle-of-the-Road
KORJ	94.3	Adult Contemporary
KOST	103.5	Beautiful Music
KOTE	106.3	Beautiful Music
KPCS*	89.3	Educational
KPFK*	90.7	Educational
KROQ	106.7	Album-Oriented Rock
KRTH	101.1	Adult Contemporary
KSAK*	90.1	Educational
KSBR*	88.5	Educational
KSPC*	88.7	Educational
KSRF	103.1	Middle-of-the-Road
KSUL*	90.1	Educational
KUCI*	89.9	Educational
KUNF*	88.3	Educational
KUSC*	91.5	Educational
KUTE	101.9	Adult Rhythm & Blues/Disco
KWIZ	96.7	Soft Contemporary
KWST	105.9	Album-Oriented Rock
KWVE	107.9	Middle-of-the-Road
KXLU*	88.9	Educational
KYMS	106.3	Contemporary Christian
KZLA	93.9	Album-Oriented Rock

*Noncommercial.
Source: Broadcasting Yearbook, 1979; updated by the Los Angeles Times Marketing Research Department to reflect format changes as of June 1979.

cisco popular music station KYA in the early sixties, Donahue had been responsible for a loosening up of the range of music played and had a hand in the promotion of concerts through which the cadre of world-famous San Francisco musicians of the 1960s emerged.

Donahue had started in radio in Philadelphia had been implicated in the payola scandals of the later 1950s. Transferred to KMPX, a loosely jazz station, Donahue helped do two things: give FM radio a broad-based popularity as a carrier of music; and establish the idea of "underground" radio—meaning a format involving a wide degree of freedom in what music with youth appeal was played. KMPX flourished until 1967–68; after a strike the staff moved en bloc to another half-redundant station on the local FM band, KSAN.[8]

KSAN emerged from the underground as a very successful album-oriented station with unobtrusive advertisements and a high degree of audience identification. By the later 1970s, however, its owners, the Metromedia chain, were unhappy with its competitive position. We spoke in 1979 to Jerry Graham, its general manager. Graham noted, "KSAN has evolved from a totally free-form radio station—by free-form I mean an entirely new brand of music and disc jockeys among whom there was a cultural bond. One based on drugs and anti-war sentiment. It could not last. We think and plan a lot more; we have structures and frameworks. But we are still the freest station in America." (Graham was ousted shortly after to make way for change.) KSAN's evolution is closely paralleled by that of the original San Francisco concert promoter and club owner, Bill Graham (no relation): for his presentational work the man will have a place in most histories of West Coast popular music.

The Bay Area's reputation as the home of alternatives is in part justified, in part another facet of the San Francisco myth described earlier. *Rolling Stone* magazine, like KSAN, grew up—and its publisher Jan Wenner took it to New York, a better publishing center. The *Berkeley Barb*, symbol of student revolt at the University of California campus at Berkeley across the Bay from San Francisco, survives, but the paper, which had its

8. Susan Krieger, *Hip Capitalism.*

finest hour when there were riots in Berkeley over the "People's Park" in 1969, is much changed. It became in the 1970s a free paper carrying advertisements for pornography and prostitution, and now, cleansed, its radicalism is formula-based and lacks conviction. Better is *Mother Jones,* published in San Francisco at a middle-income cover price ($1.50), while calling itself a magazine for the people and devoted to exposing the CIA, and the auto manufacturers. *The Reader* in San Diego is one of the best examples, along with the *San Francisco Bay Guardian,* as an alternative to the available newspapers: both pursue a fairly level-headed commercial policy.

Few of the Californian alternatives, whatever their political stripe, have escaped being influenced by the state's two Pacifica Foundation stations, KPFA FM in Berkeley and KPFK FM in the Los Angeles listening area. Lewis Hill, a liberal visionary in the Upton Sinclair tradition, was an ex-journalist in the Bay Area in the 1940s with an idea for an alternative to commercial radio, and an alternative to wire service news—held to be controlled by "sponsors and interests . . . seldom sympathetic toward fundamental labor problems." The basis for the blend of folk music, jazz, classical music, high-brow talk that KPFA produced was a new idea; sponsorship by listeners themselves (plus a Ford Foundation grant and a transmitter donated to the station by Raytheon).

KPFA started broadcasting in 1949 and its audience has never been large—its 1980 subscription list was only 10,500. But it made up in controversy for what it lacked in listeners and was investigated several times by Congressional committees anxious about the loyalty of its staff to the United States. A broadcast in 1959 by Marxist Herbert Aptheker brought down the subcommittee in internal security of the U.S. Senate Judiciary Committee to investigate Pacifica: a local professor called Samuel Hayakawa (later U.S. Senator in a decidedly illiberal mould) was active in organizing protests on behalf of the station. KPFA survived obscenity charges and constant challenges through the FCC before expanding its operations to launch a parallel station in Los Angeles, KPFK; and stations in New York (WBAI) and Houston. KPFA's proximity during the 1960s to the site of Berkeley's great events kept it in the line of criticism: *Barron's* magazine accused it in 1970 of fomenting the "People's Park" riots the previous year. Later, the station was the first to receive messages from the abductors of Patty Hearst. But nowadays, general manager Warren Van Orden told us, the "political edge" has gone. The station has had problems with labor unions and fights a perennial battle for enough money to keep going. It is the constant target of minority groups' complaints that they do not receive sufficient programing. Yet the station survives, possibly because the San Francisco area still abounds, as founder Lewis Hill once said, with coops, colleges, and cultural institutions. And KPFA still remains, in the words of radical journalist Larry Bensky (who has worked at various times for KSAN), "one of the few workable alternatives to the established media structure in Northern California."

The New Media Future

The "new media" such as cable and cassette recorder pose big problems for local television news and for local radio. California, as a receiving center for the media, has been both ahead of and behind the rest of the nation. San Diego—mainly because of its mountains—has long been the national leader among large urban centers in the proportion of its homes hooked up to cable; this has greatly increased the proportion of San Diego homes watching Los Angeles television channels—and makes the entire region of southern California into a laboratory for anyone who wishes to study multi-channel television competition.

While the various formats of both cable and video playback must greatly affect television, we believe that their impact on radio may also be profound. There is the general point that hit parade and popular music will in the future be more readily available in two new video forms—music-and-video via both cable and home playback (casette or disc). Second, these new media also include two-way possibilities of communication, such as QUBE—which, not accidentally, has been operated by Warner, a music business giant. This potentially suggests that two-way cable will be especially suitable for testing material before it is marketed. If so it may have major implications not just for the Los Angeles record industry but for the central role which radio-play and radio hit-lists have to date had in popular music.

An obvious possibility in popular music is that the pattern of record industry fragmentation in the 1960s followed by concentration in the 1970s will be repeated with the new media in the future.

In news also there appears to be a danger that the current extremes of *national* network news and very *local* city tabloid-style news—as in both TV and radio news today—will continue. The political economy of the state may get lost between the space satellite up above and the cable snaking between the suburban palm trees down below.

7

Press

California is full of provincialism. Urban Californians often share little except a fear of earthquakes and a fierce belief in the superiority of California's weather. The *Los Angeles Times,* a major newspaper with a staff of more than 570 journalists, finds the historical city on the Bay so interesting that it stations all of two journalists in San Francisco (and they have to cover the populous Bay Area counties as well). The newspapers of that cosmopolitan city San Francisco have no permanent coverage of the 14 million people who live in Los Angeles and southern California. Even the *Sacramento Bee,* which has flatteringly been compared to the *Washington Post* for the detail of its coverage of governmental affairs in the Californian capital, had, in 1979–80, not one correspondent in Los Angeles. (It did have a half-time sports man.)

Chapter Six identified the failure of television to cover statewide politics. Newspaper coverage of politics and government is stronger, but full of gaps. In a critical article[1] Ed Salz-

1. Ed Salzman, "The New Generation of Newspapers," *California Journal,* April 1977, p. 123.

man, editor of the *California Journal* and ex-*Oakland Tribune* staffer, went around the state pointing up the holes in political coverage. Medium-sized papers ignored statewide races, he alleged. The Oakland paper, the *San Francisco Examiner,* the *Long Beach Independent,* and other major city papers had few if any staff regularly assigned to political coverage, beyond City Hall. In his autobiography, the Californian prophet of tax reduction Howard Jarvis records his amazement at what he calls the political ignorance of senior editorial staff on the *San Jose Mercury.* During a discussion with them prior to the voting on Proposition 13 in 1978, he claims that vital parts of the machinery of state government were unknown to them. Jarvis is no scholar of constitutional niceties—but his contention is made plausible by the fact that the *Mercury* had only half a correspondent actually in Sacramento at the time.[2]

California is often pictured by its boosters as the equivalent of a nation, with a regional domestic product that puts it among the world's largest. If so, it is a nation that knows remarkably little about itself: the Washington correspondent of the *San Francisco Chronicle* said he hardly knew the names of Congressmen from southern California. The same man, John Fogarty, told us of a story on agriculture he had written. The *Chronicle*'s news desk wanted to "spike" it—"no relevance to the Bay Area," the editors said. The very existence of a major Bay Area city—Concord, with a population of 100,000—was unknown throughout most of the rest of the state because it slipped the net (the *San Francisco Chronicle,* the "metropolitan" Bay Area paper, is poor on local news even for the city of San Francisco). Likewise, the huge urban agglomeration south of Los Angeles proper in Orange County and south Los Angeles is often not covered. Orange County has no commercial television stations; and an obscure but highly profitable local paper, *The Register,* is the dominant source of Orange County news.

What holds California together in news are the news agencies. The Associated Press bureau in Sacramento is said to be one of the best in any state capital. United Press International

2. Howard Jarvis, *I'm Mad as Hell.*

is strong in California. But the state of California's 280,000 employees, the assembly, and the senate have to be covered by AP's seven-man Sacramento bureau—which also covers the northern part of the Central Valley. For those papers—declining in number—which take both AP and UPI services, California-wide news probably comes through in greatest volume: AP's headquarters bureau is in Los Angeles, while UPI's is in San Francisco, so taken together both services provide optimal coverage of the major urban areas. Reeve Hennion, UPI's western regional editor, told us the agencies were in "head to head" competition and regularly monitored which papers of those taking both services used which agency in print.

Small community papers in California which do not take even AP's or UPI's intra-state wire service rely on a specialist Sacramento news bureau for stories sent out by mail. Capitol News Service packages handouts and legislative reports, concentrating on state news of interest to localities. One of the company's news editors, Bob Davidson, intimated to us that it was pretty much a shoestring operation; he "couldn't afford" to subscribe to the *Los Angeles Times*—despite the *Times*'s generally acknowledged excellence in coverage of state politics.

Thus Sacramento, interesting enough to the five hundred or so registered lobbyists who throng its legislative halls, is only fitfully in the news. Bob Egelko, of AP's Sacramento bureau, told us that he and colleagues were consciously weak on fiscal politics: which may have been one reason for the sudden discovery by the population of California in 1978 that their property tax system was seriously out of kilter and needed Proposition 13 to set it right.

Journalists are generally critical people, and those we spoke to often blamed the parsimony of their employers for not mounting a fuller coverage. An editor of the *San Francisco Examiner* cited the absence of political news from Los Angeles in her paper. The city editor of the *Chronicle,* David Perlman, stated his laudable ambition to beef up the paper's coverage of state and federal governmental impact in the area, but the *Chronicle*'s publishers would have to expand their news-gathering operation in order to realize his dream. Senior editors, however, in both San Francisco and Los Angeles showed signs of being entirely satisfied with their papers' newsgathering—a situation, it seems, reflecting the absence of any competition from either California television or other newspapers. Bill Thomas, editor of the *Los Angeles Times,* told us outright: "I don't think much about competiton." At the *San Francisco Chronicle,* Bill German, the managing editor, said his journalists got vestigial competition from the *San Francisco Examiner;* but this was about all. "I suppose we could try to compete on a level with the *Los Angeles Times,* but we are not addressing the same public. The *Los Angeles Times* has chosen to go several steps beyond the level we have chosen to remain at."

Such sentiments are naturally not confined to California (although Bill German's complacency provides a clue to why the Bay Area—home of world-famous universities, high technology industry, and a population base of 5 million plus—cannot sustain a top class newspaper). They raise a general point about American newspapers. In the absence of editorial competition, what are the sources of stimulus and change within newspapers? California provides an interesting answer in two parts: powerful publishers and the search for newspaper profitability in a stratified urban marketplace. California's two big urban areas, Los Angeles and San Francisco Bay, are testing grounds for the "umbrella" theory of press competition[3] linking major metropolitan papers (e.g., the *Chronicle*) with citywide papers (e.g., the *San Jose Mercury*) and community papers (e.g., the *San Mateo Times*) through a series of overlapping and marginally competitive circles. Some California papers cannot be understood outside the exceptional history of the state.

California Dynasts

Newspapers, for most of California's press history, have commonly been run by rich men as much for political purposes as for money-making. And the wealth of newspapers owners has usually come from California's prime source: land. The Spreckels family who once owned papers in San Francisco and San Diego were sugar tycoons. The Otis and Chandler families

3. See Bruce Owen, *Economics and Freedom of Expression,* Cambridge, Mass., 1975.

of Los Angeles (the present boss of the *Times* carrying both names) owned real estate; they took an aggressive part in making the city and its land values grow. Such was the Copley dynasty of San Diego. The Copley family is a splendid example of how many mistakes you can afford to make in the newspaper business, so long as you have first made one really sound decision. The one sound decision was made in 1928 by Ira C. Copley when he bought San Diego's morning *Union* and afternoon *Tribune* from the Spreckels family. Copley was a utilities magnate and newspaper owner from northwest Illinois. His San Diego monopoly allowed him to make a series of disastrous decisions with a string of different Los Angeles suburban papers; he spent much of the 1930s cruising on a lavish yacht. The dynasty's scions, like Ira's successor, James, were adopted sons. James Copley, friend of Richard Nixon and allegedly of the CIA, gave his papers their reputation of political extremism. He died in 1973, leaving an unsound will, a chain of newspapers, and major inheritance tax problems to his second wife and former secretary, Helen. Mrs. Copley has since done for the San Diego dailies roughly what Otis Chandler in the early 1960s did for the *Los Angeles Times:* she brought them back from the far right, appointed intelligent editors, and so on. The *San Diego Union* under editor Gerald Warren (one of the few Nixon aides to escape with his reputation intact) has today some claim to being one of the better papers in the United States. It is the flagship of a Copley empire which includes a nationally important syndication service with some 1500 daily and weekly newspaper clients.

In the north of the state, the three great dynasties are those of San Francisco, Sacramento, and Oakland—the last once one of the state's premier cities, now fallen a peg or two. The dynasty's heyday was the forty years after World War I when California newspapers wielded a remarkable political power. The *Oakland Tribune,* under its owners the Knowland family, enjoyed a rare strength. After Joseph "Silk Hat" Knowland (who made his money out of Alameda County's expansion) became publisher in 1915, the paper was a stentorian voice of California Republicanism. Its owners were poised for political careers.

Old Joe's son, Bill, collected his father's political debts in 1945 when he was appointed to the United States Senate by then governor of the state Earl Warren. As a young and struggling district attorney, Earl Warren had come to the Knowlands' notice and had been pushed by them into county, then statewide politics. In its heyday the *Oakland Tribune* was a Hecht-MacArthur kind of paper, its editorial line set without demur by the publisher. Whomsoever Joseph and Bill backed, their names were plugged.

The Knowland family ownership dissolved in the mid-1970s in a fierce internecine fight over inheritance involving great-aunts and nephews. The *Tribune*'s journalists looked on at a great story they could not, of course, put in the paper.

The owners of the family paper across the Bay, the *San Francisco Chronicle,* were less politically imaginative than good at inter-marriage. Founded in the middle of the nineteenth century by Charles de Young, the *Chronicle* passed between interlocking Nob Hill families of de Youngs, Camerons, and Thieriots. Never especially strident in their Republicanism, they have been loyal to the party for over a hundred years. When the strong man of California's current delegation to the U.S. House of Representatives, Phillip Burton (whose Sixth District takes in famous tourist and multi-ethnic areas of San Francisco), first fought for election to the California state assembly from a San Francisco district, his name was completely omitted from the *Chronicle* on the publisher's instructions. But politics always seemed to take second place to drama in a paper that began life as a chronicle of the local theater and has since preferred sensational stories. Beatniks, hippies, and topless bars were the *Chronicle*'s stock in trade.

The greatest Californian dynast will always be William Randolph Hearst, still a man of unclassifiable stature in American political and media history. Hearst was one of the creators of sensational journalism. In our estimation the first great "crossover" (when he came to settle in his home state of California in the 1920s in order to concentrate on building a movie empire), Hearst owned a string of Californian papers. Two, the *San Francisco Examiner* and the Los Angeles *Herald-Examiner,* survive. The chief editor of the former, Randolph Hearst, gave a daughter to media celebrity in the kidnap and subsequent adventures of Patty Hearst.

California was not exempt from the dynastic decline evident throughout the United States since 1950: Though there is dispute over the relative strength of television and third-generation sibling rivalry as explanations. In the state, as elsewhere, ownership became concentrated. By 1980 eight ownerships altogether had two-thirds of California press sales. These included three national chains—Knight-Ridder, Gannett, and the Chicago Tribune; three California-based chains, Times-Mirror, Copley, and McClatchy; plus the surviving Hearst papers and the *San Francisco Chronicle*. California, too, had its exemplars of urban afternoon newspapers—especially vulnerable as readers fled to distant suburbs, distribution was held up by drivetime traffic, and the early evening television news presented fierce competition for the attention of the commuter once home. The two Hearst titles have been vulnerable in these ways.

Metropolitan News

California's two "megapolitan" areas have parallel features as markets for newspapers. In both areas, a single paper has pretensions to "metropolitan" status (i.e., circulated outside its original city). In both areas, the vagaries of television signal strength mean that wealthy urban areas with a municipal and commercial identity do not have any major stations—which leaves a great advertising opportunity for newspapers. We noted earlier the apparent complacency of some California editors about competition; so it is worth looking at the two urban areas to see how much commercial and editorial rivalry there is.

The leading Bay Area paper is the *San Francisco Chronicle;* its dynastic owners, the Thieriots, are incorporated in a publishing company with some out-of-state television, newspaper and radio holdings and, most controversially, with the title to the San Francisco television station KRON. A canny clan, the dynasty bought into television early; they used televison-generated money in the 1950s in a circulation battle with the *San Francisco Examiner.* The *Chronicle,* with a daily circulation of over 500,000 in 1979, won, expanded, and, now that KRON as an affiliate of NBC is doing badly, may even subsidize a television station.

San Francisco is one of the best cities in the United States in which to examine two media policy issues of recent years: the dangers of a local combine owning both television and a newspaper; permitted agreements between newspapers in order to preserve titles that would in normal trade be outlawed. San Francisco's evidence is, first, that by and large newspaper news does not get distorted by cross-ownership. All *Chronicle* reporters told us that, while they were sensitive to stories about media regulation and especially to stories involving KRON, they had never been deflected. One man's long piece had, he noted, spent a long time "upstairs" (meaning the publisher's office), but it got printed. The *Chronicle*'s star columnist, Herb Caen, has no problem with his little digs at KRON—such as his report that delivery of the *Chronicle* to the television station had been stopped because the bill was not paid. From the KRON side, executive Steve Levin told us (not without a touch of bitterness): "I've seen no benefit from the relationship. And it is sometimes to our disadvantage to have the connection since we get no preferred treatment from the paper and a lot of opposition." Once, however, in 1968 *Chronicle* personnel were caught doing dirty work for KRON's benefit, at a time when KRON's franchise was under review. The episode made the fortune of local radical journalist Bruce Brugmann, but has not been repeated.

Whether the Newspaper Preservation Act was necessary in San Francisco is unclear. Under the Act's dispensation, the *Chronicle* and *Examiner* are bound commercially in a holding company which controls their printing, distribution, and advertising operations. Out of this strange marriage—between papers that spent the 1940s and 1950s in fierce editorial and circulation fights—was born a combined Sunday newspaper. Weekdays, the *Chronicle* (morning) and *Examiner* (afternoon) appear independently—come Sunday, they pool contributions to produce a hybrid paper looking like the *Examiner* up front,

146   MEDIA MADE IN CALIFORNIA

but with the back of the book supplied by the *Chronicle*. William L. Rivers, a Stanford University observer of the Bay Area press, noted[4] that the Sunday *"Exonicle"* lacks specific character. The Newspaper Preservation Act has worked to cushion the *Examiner:* with circulation around 150,000 and dropping, the *Examiner* fails to plug the numerous gaps in urban news gathering left by the *Chronicle*'s regional ambitions. Only one-fifth of the *Chronicle*'s circulation was in 1979 within the city of San Francisco—thus it qualifies as a metropolitan paper. It competes in some measure with suburban daily newspapers such as the *Peninsula Times-Tribune,* a recent merger of the Palo Alto and Redwood City papers and owned by the Chicago Tribune Company. But the *Chronicle*'s identity remains in the city it has commercially abandoned. Witness Herb Caen, who half-consciously peddles a daily diet of local mythology—conjuring up for a suburban audience a city that once was, or once imagined, but no longer is. Caen writes about a San Francisco of cable cars and fine architecture. Reality is a city of corporate high rise, undistinguishable from others, in which real tensions—such as that between the gay community and the ethnic whites—swell and occasionally erupt.

Though Herb Caen might be ranked with Art Buchwald and Russell Baker as having established a unique journalistic "voice," Caen does not survive syndication. He is too local, like the *Chronicle* itself. It is indicative that the *Chronicle*'s three best-known columnists—Caen, Art Hoppe, and Stanton Delaplane—are masters of the light whimsical touch. The *Chronicle* lacks *gravitas.*

The *Chronicle,* according to its executives, is the paper of the whole of northern California from the Oregon border down to Santa Barbara. This is more than a slight exaggeration. To the south of the Bay, the *Chronicle*'s executives have studiously avoided anything like competiton with the powerful Knight-Ridder chain's *San Jose Mercury-News.*

The *Chronicle*'s undistinguished Washington reporting results from its miserly one-man bureau there. It also has downright poor coverage of California-wide politics and anything to

4. William L. Rivers and David M. Rubin, *A Region's Press.*

do with the 14 million people who live around and beyond Los Angeles. The *Chronicle* is a provincial paper in a provincial city. And maybe the northern Californians like it that way. They have twice been offered the opportunity of a more ambitious kind of newsaper; once in the 1950s by the virtuoso *Chronicle* editor Paul Smith, who had ambitions but no publisher to back him. Then in 1962–64 the *New York Times* briefly attempted a West Coast edition, which failed miserably in the Bay Area and elsewhere.

One step down from the *Chronicle* are two Bay Area papers with a 150,000-plus circulation. Across the Bay, Oakland has always presented a harder face to the world than San Francisco: it was where the Southern Pacific Railroad established its terminus, where Henry Kaiser (the construction magnate and wartime shipbuilder/industrialist) made and bequeathed a fortune, where the docks still flourish and hope to receive the China trade of the 1980s. Its newspaper and its owner, likewise. When the Knowland dynasty fell apart, the paper passed in rapid succession through the hands of Combined Communications Corp. into those of Gannett. The chain has since early 1979 installed the paper's first black editor, arrested the falling circulation, and launched an early morning edition called *East Bay Today,* which effectively makes the *Tribune* a 24-hour paper. The signs are that Gannett will push the *Tribune* and reduce the *Chronicle*'s circulation in the East San Francisco Bay.

With its circulation over 210,000 and growing in a still rapidly expanding community, the *San Jose Mercury-News* (the combination of the morning *Mercury* and the afternoon *News*) is one of the strongest papers in the state. California journalism abounds with predictions of the *Mercury-News*'s evolution into the major Bay Area paper—predictions which seem to us remarkably sanguine. The *Mercury-News* has grown rapidly from its 1959 combined circulation of 116,000, but its growth has been fueled by a commercial fact specific to San Jose—and one that will not carry the paper far outside Santa Clara County. The Bay Area is a single "area of dominant influence" for television signals that emanate—in the case of the major network-affiliated stations—from San Francisco. Local advertisers in San Jose either pay San Francisco television rates and get

TABLE 7.1 California's Larger Daily Newspapers 1964–1979
m = morning e = evening

| | Circulation | | Percentage |
	1979 (thousands)	1964 (thousands)	Change 1964–79
LOS ANGELES AREA			
Orange Coast Daily Pilot	45e	27e	+65%
Long Beach Independent	63m	43m	+45%
Press Telegram	72e	113e	−36%
(combined m + e)	(135)	(157)	(−14%)
Los Angeles Herald Examiner	301e	730e	−59%
Los Angeles Times	1,014m	817	+24%
Pasadena Star News	51m + e	62m + e	−18%
Pomona Progress Bulletin	43m + e	40e	+8%
Riverside Enterprise	65m	31m	+106%
Press	34e	33e	+2%
(combined)	(98)	(64)	(+53%)
San Bernardino Sun	81m	71m + e	+13%
San Gabriel Valley Daily Tribune	66m + e	66e	−1%
Santa Ana Register	220m + e	91m + e	+141%
Santa Barbara Press News	45e	35e	+29%
Torrance Daily Breeze	84e	37e	+126%
Van Nuys Valley News	230m [1]	—	—
Los Angeles La Opinion	37m	15m	+147%
SAN FRANCISCO BAY AREA			
Hayward Daily Review	43e	33e	+30%
Oakland Tribune	165e	207e	−20%
Palo Alto Peninsula Times Tribune	63e	41e	+54%
San Francisco Chronicle	505m	351m	+44%
San Francisco Examiner	158e	301m	−48%
San Mateo Times & News Leader	45e	33e	+40%
San Jose Mercury	150m	90m	+67%
News	66e	64e	+4%
(combined)	(216)	(154)	(+41%)
San Rafael Independent Journal	45e	36e	+27%
Santa Rosa Press Democrat	62e	40e	+57%
Walnut Creek Contra Costa Times	101m [2]	19	+442%
Wall Street Journal western edition	316m	148m	+112%
SAN DIEGO AREA			
San Diego Union	203m	116m	+74%
Tribune	131e	117e	+11%
(combined)	(333)	(234)	(+43%)

	Circulation		Percentage
	1979 (thousands)	1964 (thousands)	Change 1964–79
CENTRAL VALLEY AREA			
Bakersfield Californian	67e	45e	+48%
Fresno Bee	124m	110e	+12%
Modesto Bee	63m	41e	+54%
Sacramento Bee	186m	170e	+10%
Sacramento Union	106m	55m	+92%
Stockton Record	56e	59e	−5%
CALIFORNIAN DAILIES	1979	1964	1964–79 Change
Number of A.M. dailies	29	20	+45%
Number of P.M. dailies	95	112	−15%
A.M. ciculation (thousands)	3,337	2,143	+56%
P.M. circulation	2,598	3,360	−23%
Daily circulation	5,935	5,503	+8%

[1] Half paid and half free distribution in 1979; in 1964 entirely free distribution.
[2] In 1979 only 48,000 of this was paid circulation; in 1964 the *Contra Costa Times* published four days a week.
Source: *Editor and Publisher Yearbook,* 1965 and 1980.

potential buyers they do not need in Oakland and Petaluma or they buy space in the *Mercury-News.* In 1977 the *Mercury-News* ran 82 million lines of advertising. Under the Ridder family, the *Mercury-News* looked like "the Yellow Pages with News." Under its present owners, the Knight-Ridder chain, its editorial quality has grown. But few Californian journalists yet rate it as better than an improving local paper. At present the combined *Mercury-News* is a leader in one field only—in the quantity of its total annual advertising linage.

Game Show Information? Newspapers in Los Angeles

Maxene Fabe[5] turned up a 1950 producer of television game shows (unnamed) who compared, unfavorably, the contestants he got in California with those in New York. "It's not that contestants are less intelligent in California," he said. "It's just that they don't seem to care about certain kinds of information. In

5. Maxene Fabe, *TV Game Shows.*

New York, what you talk about is provided for you by the *New York Times.*" The judgment is dated, for two reasons. The *Los Angeles Times* is now the strong agenda-setter for the quotidian life of southern California in the same way that the *New York Times* was, and is, in New York. Whatever the *Los Angeles Times* was in the 1950s, it is now a world-class newspaper of often overwhelming physical size (about 120 pages per weekday); although only a quarter of this is non-advertising matter, the paper does have a wide range of foreign and national news. Whether game-show contestants are among its daily readership of two million is another matter.

The extent to which a single newspaper dominates public existence probably has no equivalent in any other world city as large as Los Angeles. In every respect—prestige, influence, news coverage, circulation, profit—it towers above California's second daily, the *San Francisco Chronicle.* The paper has an important function in ordering the perceptions of professional politicians and bureaucrats in Sacramento, where it is read by the elite.

In Los Angeles—and nearly as much in California at large—until it's in the *Los Angeles Times* it hasn't happened. In the world of Johnny Carson the *Times* maps the events, minutiae, opinions that he retails to America.

The *Los Angeles Times* may be an example of where the rest of the country is headed—a completely dominant daily in an urban area of some ten million people. By 1980 the circulation of its only rival, the Hearst-owned *Los Angeles Herald-Examiner,* had shrunk to less than one-third that of the *Times,* while its advertising revenue must be less than one-tenth. While the *Herald-Examiner*'s circulation is confined to central and northwest Los Angeles, the *Times* covers the huge urban area from San Diego north to Palmdale.

Compared with other major metropolitan dailies, the *Times* has gone further in combining sections within the paper and producing special sections going to different areas. Two outlying areas, Orange County and San Diego, have since 1978 received a special local section each day. Six other areas receive a local section once a week. A major satellite printing plant in Orange County is being followed by another in the San Fernando Valley. The 500-plus page Sunday edition has a bewildering array of sections. It is an extreme case of a general truth: mammoth Sunday editions are major contributors to the advertising (and editorial) strength of larger American newspapers.

The *Los Angeles Times* daily enters about 30 percent of the households in greater Los Angeles. Its readership is heavily biased toward upper and middle income families and also upper- and middle-age brackets. Over half its sale is either in the richer northwest quadrant (the San Fernando Valley and around Beverly Hills) or in heavily WASP Orange County. Its weakest household penetration is the inner south and east areas.

The *Times* is very proud of its status. Proud also of its future prospects. It is somewhat less proud about its dynastic past. The editor, William Thomas, told us that the *Times* is rightfully number two in the land and that the *Washington Post* only managed to slip into second place "because of Watergate." Overtaking the *New York Times* is more difficult "because it has more of a tradition."

As in many successful enterprises, the past haunts the present. Robert Gottlieb and Irene Wolt's *Thinking Big* condemns the Chandler dynasty as robber barons roughly like those of northern California who made San Francisco a by-word for municipal corruption in the later nineteenth century. The Chandler dynasty, according to these authors, operated through real estate; and the *Los Angeles Times* was used as a political lobbying and publicity instrument for building and profiteering from vast housing developments, including, incidentally, Hollywood. The newspaper was also an instrument in the repression of trade unions.

David Halberstam [6] goes over this ground with emphasis on how the *Times* successfully catapulted Richard Nixon to political stardom in four elections between 1946 and 1952. Halberstam also gives emphasis to the dynastic role of Dorothy "Buff" Chandler. ("Buff" was a member of the Buffum Department Store family of Long Beach, which is entirely appropriate in

6. David Halberstam, *The Powers That Be.*

view of the massive dependence of the *Times* on department store advertising.) Buff has long been, as mentioned in Chapter Four, the presiding queen of Los Angeles musical, cultural, and social life. The way in which Dorothy Chandler used the power of the paper to bludgeon her cultural projects into existence is not regarded as embarrassing or inconsistent with the independence of a great paper. This is California, not the effete East. If you've got it, you can still flaunt it, at least in culture.

The period around 1960 was an important one in the history of the *Los Angeles Times*. Otis Chandler was made publisher at age thirty-three. By many standards a rather conventional rich young man, Otis Chandler, with his associates, quickly began to make the *Times* into a prestige paper and to do this within a more profitable and financially secure company.

1962 was a key year. In that year Richard Nixon ran for governor of California, but the *Los Angeles Times* (although endorsing Nixon editorially) for the first time in its history gave equal news treatment to the Democrat incumbent Pat Brown— who won. In Nixon's famous diatribe against the media on the night of his defeat he specifically accused the *Los Angeles Times* of being against him. Some people see this paranoid response to even-handed press coverage as a key California signpost on Nixon's road to Watergate.

Los Angeles, which until 1954 had had five metropolitan dailies, suddenly switched in 1962 from four to only two dailies. Otis Chandler thus found himself in 1962 with a morning monopoly, an event well "ahead of its time" for a city the size of Los Angeles. Chandler has been consistently fortunate in the incompetence of Hearst management. Two years later, in 1964, the *Herald-Examiner*, with its afternoon monopoly, was only behind by 730,000 to the *Times*'s 817,000. But television was already hurting afternoon sales, especially in Los Angeles, with its drive-commuter pattern.

The *Herald-Examiner* then made bad worse. While the *Los Angeles Times* (without unions) raised salaries, the Hearst management (with unions) tried to hold them down. The American Newspaper Guild—not a militant labor union—was stung into action. A strike/lockout begun in 1967, dragged on for an incredible seven years in all. The *Herald-Examiner* continued to appear, but the journalists who were willing to cross the picket lines and to accept the low pay were not the most illustrious of their profession. The paper sank. In 1978 a completely new strategy was adopted: produce a bright, lively afternoon paper aimed at the affluent young of west and northwest Los Angeles.

If Hearst has been one stroke of fortune for the Chandlers, another was the mediocrity (until about the mid-1970s) of most of its suburban competition both editorially and commercially. Despite much talk about the relentless drive of the new suburban press, the only moderately well-run suburban competition has, until recently, been the Orange County *Register,* and its policy of doing everything on the cheap allowed the *Times* to capture the affluent top end of that market.

Thus, in 1980, the *Los Angeles Times* can afford to take the expansive line it favors in its corporate publicity. It is, after all, the world's fattest newspaper; a national leader in newspaper advertising; the major profit center of the Times-Mirror Company which owns it, and which itself is the largest public corporation owning major newspapers in the United States. Through the news service it provides jointly with the *Washington Post,* it now has a national presence. Through Times-Mirror it has sister papers in the Dallas *Times Herald* and *Newsday* on Long Island, New York.

Are there no clouds on this southern California horizon? The *Times* still somehow lacks in character, both political and geographical. The *Times* no longer makes endorsements for President, or in California for governor or U.S. Senator. It endorses for all the lesser offices, choosing a mixture of Democrats and Republicans for individual merit. Its general editorial policy is similar. It has opinions and publishes editorials on a wide range of controversial issues. By favoring lesser individuals while avoiding party labels, the *Times* unintentionally contributes to the fragmentation of California politics.

Usually it does not deeply commit itself on the major issues that are controversial in Los Angeles and California. Especially it does not wheel out in pursuit of editorial policies its own favored weapons—long investigative features zig-zagging in parallel across page after page. The editors consider it must be cautious about how it uses its power. Certainly its power is such that when it is used—for example, in its coverage of conflict within the California Supreme Court in November 1978—the results can be embarrassingly sudden and dramatic. Nevertheless prestige papers establish their prestige by committing themselves on big and risky issues. The *Times* has won Pulitzer Prizes, and its Washington bureau was second only to the *Post* in the early Watergate pursuit. But for the *Los Angeles Times* Watergate was not a hometown story.

The other cloud on the *Times*'s horizon is near to home. Just as the Times-Mirror's own *Newsday* and its papers in Connecticut provide some of the *New York Times*'s own more vigorous competition, so there will be more of the same in Los Angeles. It is not clear whether the *Los Angeles Times* will be able to go on beating back all of the suburbans at once while still making such a big profit. Nor is it clear that a newspaper's fatness always means health. The physical size of the *Times* (which results partly from low advertising line rates which compete with the suburbans) causes enormous logistic problems. One problem is that, despite "local" editions, outside the metropolitan area the reader gets rather little local news. Meanwhile readers received a newspaper of which only 24 percent is nonadvertising matter.*

Recent purchases by the national newspaper chains of Los Angeles suburban papers indicate competition is in the offing—its umbrella may be punctured. At present the *Times* competes and co-habits with some twenty local dailies in the various municipalities that make up the greater Los Angeles/ Orange counties area. The Times-Mirror Company owns one, the *Orange Coast Daily Pilot;* it was forced by court order to divest itself of another in San Bernardino.

The *Times* overlap with these suburban papers varies: but most Los Angeles households take either one daily or none. For example, of households in southwest Los Angeles which in 1978 took the local *Daily Breeze,* only 25 percent also took the

---

* In contrast to 42 percent and 30 percent in the *New York Times* and *Washington Post* in 1979. *Editor and Publisher,* March 15, 1980.

Los Angeles Times. Moreover the competition is not direct; one is a local afternoon paper which lives up to its title; the other is a morning metropolitan paper.

Some *Times* executives were, in 1979–80, most anxious about a "new" suburban title in the San Fernando Valley. The *Valley News,* formerly a give-away, is now being aggressively promoted by its new owners, the Chicago Tribune chain. This chain, Bill Thomas, the *Times*'s editor, told us, believes in putting out good papers and should do something with the *Valley News.* But these and the other suburbans will remain local, he insists, and so be unable to compete either editorially or in metropolis-wide advertising. And *Times* resources permit it aggression as well as defense. Its San Diego local pages have brought some competition to the Copley empire based on the *San Diego Union* and *Tribune.* Gerald Warren, the *Union*'s editor, impressed us by launching into a passionate description of his paper's editorial superiority over the *Times.* In fact, competition probably hinges more on the practical facts of newspaper delivery than editorial quality—a consideration the "umbrella" theorists often miss. Three-quarters of *Los Angeles Times* circulation is home delivered—no other paper in the world daily home delivers 750,000 papers of such bulk over such an enormous distance. The increased fuel costs of delivery were one argument in favor of the second satellite printing plant for the San Fernando Valley.

California's Oddest of Newspapers

There can be few newspapers in the United States stranger than the Orange County *Register.* In 1979 its daily sale was 220,000, and it carried the ninth largest number of advertising lines in the country. On some weekdays, it has more pages than the *Los Angeles Times,* yet few Californians outside Orange County have heard of this remarkable newspaper.

The *Register,* based in Santa Ana, looks and reads like a small community newspaper. It is packed with very local news about each of the main communities within Orange County, that sprawling, headless suburban acreage which produced the

John Birch Society. As Orange County grew very rapidly in the 1950s and 1960s toward a population of 1.8 million people in 1977, the *Register* grew with it.

The *Register* is owned by the Hoile family, who call their chain of papers the Freedom Group. They are libertarians. Orange County may be nationally known for staunch Republicanism, but the *Register* does not support Republicans of any kind. The *Register* is against all political parties and against all politicians (unless retired or, better still, dead) for the very logical reason that it is against politics. Politicians are bad, and, despite some stirrings of right-wing loyalty, the *Register* was first to reveal the dubious financial arrangements by which Richard Nixon had paid for his "western White House" in San Clemente, the Orange County beach resort.

The *Register* cares about liberty and Orange County, pays its journalists badly, tolerates no labor unions, and is barely interested in any news from Sacramento, let alone Washington. In 1978 when San Diego had the worst disaster to date in domestic U.S. aviation history, the *Register* did not send a single reporter on the 90-minute drive down the freeway. San Diego is not in Orange County.

But the *Register* succeeds because its space is cheap. Like San Jose in the north, Orange County lacks a big television station of its own, and advertisers wanting to reach only a local market find it uneconomic to pay the area-wide rates of the major stations. So the *Register,* unimaginatively presented, its editorial philosophy extreme, its journalism mediocre, gets the advertisements—and Orange County readers.

California has another odd newspaper, or rather two more odd newspapers, and they are located in a rather odd news town—Sacramento. We noted earlier how a characteristic of the flow of news in the state was the relative weakness of political news, especially coming from the state capital. Yet within Sacramento itself there is the odd circumstance of two newspapers of comparable size locked in competition, each producing some of the best informed local and statewide political coverage available in California. No other editor remarked to us, as did Bob Carney of the Sacramento *Union,* that he relished competition with the other local paper, the *Sacramento Bee,* on the grounds that "it keeps the reporters on their toes."

The Sacramento *Union* is a morning paper with a daily circulation of 106,000 (in 1979); fully computerized, like its competitor, it runs on a fairly tight cost schedule, with 85 percent of its circulation within the greater Sacramento urban area. Of the California papers it has one of the most attractive layouts. It has recently begun to pick up department store advertising from the hitherto dominant *Bee.* There is no reason, says Bob Carney, why two papers cannot both survive (even though this would buck the all-over America trend of the past 30 years toward one-paper cities). The *Union's* problem is not commercial but managerial. Formerly owned by Copley, it became part of the Panax empire, in which the controversial entrepreneur John McGoff had a leading part. McGoff was involved, abortively, in bidding for the *Washington Star;* he was involved, allegedly, in an attempt by the government of the Republic of South Africa to buy American newspaper influence. In 1980, Panax was bought up by the multi-national Thomson organization, through its Canadian headquarters: the future of the *Union* remains unclear.

By contrast, the *Bee* has been blessed by five generations of fairly steady publishers, belonging to a Scotch-Presbyterian clan which settled in Sacramento in gold-rush days, the McClatchys. The *Bee* is a Sacramento institution like the old Senator Hotel across from the capitol where the deals are traditionally made; it is another branch of California state government. But here's the paradox: the *Bee* is an enlightened, liberal newspaper. Unionized, it pays its journalists well and has recruited a fine set of writers. Its publisher C. K. McClatchy once worked on Adlai Stevenson's staff. He is capitalist enough to run lucrative television and radio stations as well as the *Bee;* but liberal enough to set his journalists in Fresno free to fight the growers of the Central Valley.

The McClatchy clan has built a little empire over the years. The *Sacramento Bee* has junior sisters in Modesto and Fresno— separate editorial entities which take their national and international news, plus features and some editorials, from Sacramento via computer-backed transmission lines. McClatchy has recently bought into the Alaskan press.

The clan's flagship is the *Sacramento Bee*. Circulation 186,-000 (in 1979), the paper's market extends north as far as the Oregon border. And west; but it is not sold any nearer San Francisco than Vacaville, a fruit-growing town with the dubious distinction of holding Charles Manson in its state prison. A "gentleman's agreement," says the *Bee*'s managing editor, Frank McCullough, stops it competing with the *San Francisco Chronicle*. In 1978 the *Bee* switched from afternoon to morning, causing the *Union* to file suit, believing the move to be a bid to crush its market. Not so, says McCullough—"we could be in a new era when low-cost computer technology permits two papers of this size to survive."

Umbrellas in California

The umbrella theory of the press sees the dominant metropolitan daily as competing with the major suburban dailies, which in turn compete with the small suburban papers, which in turn compete with the "community" press. This is a comforting theory, but we believe it ignores some simple realities. There is less competition, we believe, than the umbrella theory supposes. In some cases there are gentleman's agreements not to compete; the metropolitan daily is a morning paper, whereas the suburban dailies are mainly afternoon papers; the metro daily is read broadly by the top one-third in terms of income and education, while the suburban afternoon papers are read mainly by the broad middle sector of the white population. In the meanwhile—at least in California—it would appear that one-third or more of all adults (and most minority adults) seldom or never read a daily newspaper. Finally, while some small suburban dailies are in highly competitive situations, the bulk of the suburban sale goes to deeply entrenched dailies which have only modest competition, carry enormous quantities of advertising, and make high profits; the extent to which other newspaper chains believe these papers to be monopolies earning monopoly profits is indicated by the mammoth prices often paid when relatively small dailies change hands. In the news on

California radio and television, competition in the major urban areas tends toward an extreme (although much of the competition is with non-news entertainment). In the state's newspapers the extreme is of a different kind—the absence of competition.

8

"Posing" for Office

"In the Golden West," said newspaper columnist Marquis Childs, "you do not run for office, you pose." In 1966, when Ronald Reagan first ran for the governorship of California, Tom Wicker (then Washington bureau chief of the *New York Times*) wrote with disdain of Reagan's "coming out of a long seclusion as a sort of two-tone sports job. He's tailored, he's painted, and he's produced for the camera."[1]

Wicker was wrong, taken in by the very public relations presentation of Reagan's candidacy he despised. California tradition is to present candidates as new fresh products: this was how Reagan was sold in 1966, in contrast to the tired, old incumbent, Governor Pat Brown. The eastern columnists did not know California. Reagan was not the first successful politician to arrive in Sacramento having made use of Hollywood techniques; nor even the first to have transmuted a reputation based on film and television celebrity into political appeal. "Image" was important before Reagan; even before the celebrated

1. Tom Wicker, "Television in the Political Campaign," *Television Quarterly*, Vol. V, No. 1, Winter 1966, p. 13.

California campaign managers Clem Whitaker and Leone Baxter began grooming candidates in the 1930s.

Reagan's critics have confused his mastery of political imagery with his conservative ideology. They have been content to condemn him for being the truly modern politician whose instincts are those of the sound stage rather than the hustings. All politicians are tyro thespians, and none more so than Richard M. Nixon, in his Californian youth a gifted and enthusiastic amateur actor. The performing skills of Reagan's successor as California governor are apparent. Edmund G. Brown, Jr. (Jerry Brown to the world) has "the right instincts for television, his highly developed sense of drama, of timing, dramatic timing." So we were informed in 1979 by Howard Gingold, press secretary to the man who at the time seemed destined to follow Brown as governor, Leo McCarthy, speaker of the California assembly. Gingold admitted that McCarthy, an accomplished legislator, was no "television natural"; he was having to learn the skills late in his political career. Without them there is no possibility of succeeding in statewide races in California. In few other states is such a premium put on the politician's mastery of presentation. In no other state has the industry which trades on the techniques of presentation—the entertainment industry based in Beverly Hills—been so influential in politics.

The Party Machine Is Dead.
Long Live the Polling Principle

Californian politics would inevitably have looked different from most other states because of geography and size. Getting a message to concentrations of people in two major urban areas 400 miles apart, while not forgetting the remainder of a large state, was always going to be expensive. The organs of communication would surely have played a big part in California politics even if political parties had been stronger. But in California, political parties have since 1910 been conspicuously weak.

At the end of the nineteenth century, the urban politics of the major population center, San Francisco, were a by-word for corruption. "Kearneyism" ruled in the city: a compound of racism, bossism, and sand-lot populism. Political arguments had a nasty tendency to end up in duels and streetfights. City politics in the emerging municipality of Los Angeles were little better, while in the rest of the state political power rested firmly with landowners and with railroad interests headed by Southern Pacific.

Reform of both city and state politics, when it came at the end of the first decade of the twentieth century, was led by Progressive-Republicans, among whom journalists played an important part. In a crusading series of articles, Edward A. Dickson of the *Los Angeles Evening Express* exposed the Southern Pacific's control of city government. Together with Chester Rowell of the *Fresno Republican*, whose desk adjoined Dickson's in the state legislature press row, Dickson formed a statewide organization under the Progressive banner called the Lincoln-Roosevelt Republican League. Their ideas for reform were typical then, as now, of journalists': a cynical view of the corrupting tendencies of political organizations married with a sentimental faith in the good sense of the common elector. The program of their league, which elected the lawyer Hiram Johnson governor in 1910, was to make state government much more responsive to the electorate's expressed will—without political party intermediaries.

In 1911 the California legislature introduced a package of reforms which—with subsequent additions—add up to a "polling principle." Because political parties could not be trusted to resist corruption the cleansing power of the popular vote must be allowed at all possible times to be directly exercised. Thus the Progressives' reforms were fourfold. A system of initiatives and propositions allowed electors to pass laws directly by majority vote. Similarly, in a referendum they could directly veto legislation; and in recall elections, they could call elected politicians to book before the normal end of their term of office. California, which had played a pioneering role in introducing primary elections, now in 1913 added yet another Progressive reform—cross-filing, which allowed candidates to run in the primaries of more than one party. Such cross-filing, which encouraged incumbents to conceal their party label, was not rescinded till 1959.

The polling principle soon became predominant in Californian politics. Later developments such as professional campaign management and sample survey polling were merely adding to the Progressives' system, in which polls of various kinds were asked to perform many of the functions that parties played elsewhere. The most active decade for initiatives (before the 1970s) was the 1930s when thirty-six state-wide initiatives qualified for the ballot. In the 1930s thirty-one other initiatives reached the stage of being "circulated" but did not pick up enough signatures to qualify. Amidst this frenzy of voting—this continuous celebration of the polling principle—parties still continued to exist as skeletal committees and caucuses. But the main channels of political communication were the newspapers. Electoral organization eventually became the specialty of an entirely new animal, the professional campaign manager. In the absence of party manifestos, personality became vital in statewide races and hence the means for conveying personality to the people. In the 1930s this was radio (as well as the press) and—California's great political innovation—the film techniques of Hollywood.

In other words, the operation of the polling principle was very expensive. Merely to qualify an initiative—the state has specialized firms that collect the signatures—cost in 1980 some $2 million. In the 1978 California election, costs amounted to a total of $58.2 million, or about $8.50 for every person who cast a vote for governor. Most of this was not spent on the governor's race itself—although Jerry Brown handsomely outspent his Republican opponent. Some of the most extravagant spending was involved in defeating Proposition 5, which would have severely restricted smoking in public places. Four tobacco companies together spent $6.1 million defending the people's right to smoke.

In such a state, little wonder that one of its most gifted politicians of recent years, Jesse Unruh, should call money "the mother's milk of politics." Or that, despite the Progressives' ambition to cleanse Sacramento, the people able to pump money into politics, lobbyists, should enjoy such a privileged place at California's legislative table.

The reformers themselves were aware of some of these implications from the outset. Hiram Johnson wrote in 1910 to his campaign manager Chester Rowell that three things had become necessary for a successful campaign: money, organization in every town and county, and "a publicity bureau in charge of a skilled and competent newspaper man." The Johnsonian prescription has held good for Californian politics ever since. The power which these reforms took from the business interests and the municipalities were transferred in part to journalists and publicists—but mainly to the people who could afford to pay them, newspaper owners and lobbyists for interests. California politics are just as ideological as anywhere else: the Johnsonian reforms led to over forty years of Republican domination. Currin V. Shields of UCLA argued in 1954 that state politics were characterized by "the tremendous advantage Republican candidates have in publicity and financial resources. In a state encompassing almost 160,000 square miles and more than 12 million people, control of mass communication is a salient feature in the political picture. The Democrats have found the one-party press in California a difficult handicap to overcome."[2]

The publisher and top political editor of one major newspaper held tremendous power. As late as 1958 would-be governor Pat Brown was calling on Kyle Palmer, political editor of the staunchly Republican *Los Angeles Times.* He had come, Brown wryly noted as he entered the Times building, to "kiss the ring." James E. Gregg found in 1966 that nonincumbents in California were more likely to win office if they had the editorial support of local newspapers.[3]

Professional Campaign Management

The strength of the polling principle in California explains why professional campaign management began there. In California,

2. Currin V. Shields in *Western Political Quarterly,* December 1954, pp. 676–77.
3. James E. Gregg "Newspaper endorsements and local elections in California," Institute of Governmental Affairs, University of California, Davis, 1966.

politics is an industry. The frequency of initiative campaigns—
local and state—ensured that there would be enough work to
keep professional campaign managers busy between the regular bi-annual elections. California's population doubled between 1920 and 1940, from 3.4 to 6.9 million—which made
keeping in touch with the electorate more difficult. The 1930s
was a significant decade. The rise of Democratic voting threatened traditional rule by the state's overwhelmingly Republican
newspapers. In 1932 President Hoover lost his home state of
California; the state also elected a Democrat as U.S. Senator.
In 1934 the governor's office could also fall to the Democrats.
The Republicans' chances dimmed when incumbent Governor
Rolph died before the election and the colorless Frank Merriam succeeded him. Re-electing Merriam was the Republican
high command's task. But the Democrats had that year solved
their chronic party problems in an unusual way. After an acri-
monious primary campaign, the winner was a celebrity, socialist
writer and journalist Upton Sinclair.

In 1934, as a writer in *Harper's* later put it, "the screen enters politics." Fearing that the eccentric but popular program
offered by Upton Sinclair could not be stopped by regular campaigning methods (such as total non-mention of Sinclair except
in the most scathing and vituperative terms in the newspapers),
Hollywood was asked by the Republicans to provide a crash
course in visual education.

More than 1.25 million people in the state were jobless and
dependent on public relief; there were large-scale strikes by
migratory workers. Farm income had halved since 1929. Into
the ferment, Sinclair, living in affluent Pasadena, injected his
formula for recovery, a program to "End Poverty in California"—municipalization and large-scale public spending. Frank-
lin D. Roosevelt, respectably established as President, was expected to endorse Sinclair (in fact he never did).

By October, Hollywood had joined the fray. Cecil B. De-
Mille announced his opposition to Sinclair. Joseph M. Schenck
declared that if Florida was wide awake enough that state
might soon gain the $150 million-a-year motion picture indus-
try. The studio bosses exacted a levy from their employees to
contribute to the Republican fighting funds organized by Re-

publican Louis B. Mayer. Sinclair was already well known in the film community—as a writer whose novels had been filmed, and as a collaborator with the Russian film director Sergei Eisenstein. In 1933 Sinclair had written a remarkable book, *Upton Sinclair Presents William Fox*. The book chronicled in great detail, with Fox's active co-operation, a murky corner of Hollywood's recent financial life. In a classic movie feud between moguls, William Fox's expansion plans had been beaten back and he himself had been ousted. One of the villains of the piece (as seen by Fox and reported by Sinclair) was Louis B. Mayer, who thus had a personal motive for wanting to get even with the socialist author. All Hollywood, however, was frightened by Sinclair, who had vague—but frequently repeated—ideas about some element of public ownership in the movie business.

For these reasons the movie moguls decided not merely to contribute financially to the anti-Sinclair campaign but to make and exhibit anti-Sinclair movies in California's movie theaters. This led to the famous fabricated newsreels, showing armies of indigents disembarking from box cars on Los Angeles railway sidings in order to get the free handouts from Governor Sinclair—and the California taxpayers.

The press also fabricated pictures. W. R. Hearst (already regretting his support for FDR in 1932 but as politically confused as ever) did not become involved in this new all-media campaigning till late in election; but then all guns blazed. The *Los Angeles Herald-Examiner* (Hearst-owned) ran a huge photograph of a frightening mob of hoboes. Close inspection revealed that the hoboes were wearing grease paint; among their number, Dorothy Wilson, Frank Darrow, and a group of actors remarkably similar to the cast of a movie called *Wild Boys of the Road*.

Upton Sinclair characteristically bounced back in 1935 with a book called, *I, Candidate for Governor and How I Got Licked*. In it he attributed his defeat to the hostility of almost all the press and almost all the radio stations (except KNX.). He was bitter about the large quantities of hostile cartoon and leaflet material handed out, and small boxed quotations (from his socialist writings—attacking, for example, the church, the family, big business) which appeared day after day on the front page of the *Los Angeles Times* and other newspapers. Sinclair still did not know, when writing a few months after his defeat, that the quotations were all selected and distributed by Clem Whitaker and Leone Baxter.

The 1934 election endorsed professional campaign management. Whitaker and Baxter played a prominent part in defeating Sinclair; this success made their reputation. The go-for-the-jugular campaign has been common in Californian politics both before and since 1934. But Whitaker and Baxter turned this kind of negative campaigning from an art into something much more systematic, more like a science.

Clem Whitaker was a Sacramento journalist turned lobbyist. He had served an apprenticeship as newspaperman for the Capitol News Bureau specializing in packaging news and tidbits from the state capital for the small local newspapers in the state. In 1933 he was hired as a publicity man on behalf of the referendum on the Central Valley Project Act—one of the state's gigantic water schemes. In the campaign he was joined by Leone Baxter, agent for the chamber of commerce in the northern California town of Redding, which had an interest in the passage of the referendum. From their combined experience of smalltown commerce and newspapers and links between these and Sacramento, they put together a package of techniques and services to be sold to an interested client—usually a corporation such as Pacific Gas and Electricity which needed voter support on a specific business/political issue. The package offered to clients included advice on placement of editorials and advertising (Whitaker and Baxter soon opened a subsidiary advertising agency) and the presentation of candidates (aligning the candidate's appearance, clothes with the campaign theme); paid volunteers for delivery; mass mailings; radio spots; billboards, etc. Whitaker and Baxter did not leave the support of the press to chance. In addition to year-round distribution of their weekly political clipsheet Californian Feature Service, they sent a complete schedule of their planned political advertisements to every paper in the state at the beginning of each campaign. To enhance this "good will," Whitaker and Baxter did not collect the regular 15 percent agency fee from the smaller papers. The overwhelmingly Republican stance of the state's press did not give the firm too great a barrier of resistance to the support of its invariably Republican clients.

And it worked. The firm undertook seventy-five Californian campaigns between 1933 and 1955—and won seventy of them. Professional campaign management and media manipulation quickly became a staple of California politics. For decades now a standard feature of the run-up to each election year has been a pairing off of candidates with hot "political consultant" professional campaign managers.

Populist Politics

The politics of misinformation has its limits, and campaign management is by no means restricted in its use to business interests or defenders of the status quo. Big labor plays the same game. In 1958, the year Pat Brown was elected governor, the San Francisco public relations firm of Leonard B. Gross and Curtis Roberts successfully managed a massive billboard and television campaign on behalf of organized labor. In 1980 a proposition that would have cut state income tax in half was defeated by the same voters who endorsed Proposition 13 and had been hailed throughout the United States as the vanguard of a new anti-tax sentiment.

Professional campaign management never replaced old-fashioned interest politics either, especially in Sacramento. As late as 1949 a peddler of influence and favors to member of the state assembly, the lobbyist Artie Samish, could proudly pose for a photograph with a dummy on his knee labelled "state assembly." It was no idle boast: Samish got the liquor, oil, land, and transport companies what they wanted.

During their successful career as campaign organizers, Whitaker and Baxter claimed their brand of popular politics had made "bossism" impossible. Bossism of the big city machine type, which existed in San Francisco at the turn of the century, had disappeared in California before campaign management arrived. Yet the 1930s and 1940s saw the apogee of a single lobbyist for a whole range of interests (Samish even represented the Holywood agents[4]). He obtained his hold over the legislators in Sacramento by channeling campaign contributions to them in return for legislative favors. Some of this campaign finance then went into campaigns managed by Whitaker and Baxter.

Art Samish's effectiveness was destroyed by an exposé, "The Secret Boss of California," in two August 1949 articles in *Collier's* (a national magazine). But this was not the end of lobbying; more like its modern beginning. After 1950, lobbying in Sacramento expanded enormously—with a much larger number of major lobbyists instead of one key lobbyist. The volume of legislation, of lobbying, of campaign contributions, and of political management-consultancy all expanded.

Professional management runs campaigns large and small. For example, judgeship elections in Los Angeles County (population 7 million); a spokesman at Cerrell Associates explained to us their winning strategy for Judge Everette E. Ricks, as a Los Angeles County superior court judge in 1978. "Down here we used his picture." (Judge Ricks is black, and "down here" was the Cerrell office not far from Watts.) But in the San Fernando Valley, where being black might lose votes, "we didn't use his picture." In Orange County the problems are different, and there is a tradition of the massive use of direct mail advertising. Robert Nelson, a political consultant based in Santa Ana, stressed his belief in spending up to 20 percent of the budget on research. A recent electoral client had been the incumbent Orange County Sheriff Brad Gates, who had been under some press suspicion of wrongdoing. The research showed that the voters liked competence, honesty, and someone who cared. The 1978 slogan thus almost wrote itself: "Brad Gates—an honest professional cop who cares." Mr. Gates won re-election.

California politics are undoubtedly populist, to the extent that "the people," albeit organized and persuaded by professionals, exercise their political will at regular intervals and on a diversity of issues. In the late 1930s the people gave a great deal of credence to a version of the Social Credit Movement advocating a revolving fund to pay vastly increased pensions: it

4. The Hollywood agents employed Art Samish in 1935 and 1937 to watch two assembly bills, for fees of $5000 and $10,000. Leo Rosten, *Hollywood,* p. 146.

went under the banner of "Ham and eggs" for breakfast for everyone every day. The utterly impractical measure was only narrowly defeated, once the big guns of political persuasion were mobilized against it. Populism rules in California in the shape of public opinion pollsters. One firm, that of Mervyn Field, is immensely influential.

The kinds of skill that politics in California demands have changed over time: Earl Warren's rather wooden smile for the still or the newsreel camera would not do nowadays. Television requires an entirely new range of attributes—some merely physical, like body size. Ed Salzman, editor of the *California Journal,* was only one of the serious-minded Californians who bewailed the fate of Jesse Unruh, former speaker of the state assembly and, in 1980, state treasurer. Unruh has had a distinguished career in California politics. But when he challenged Ronald Reagan for governor in 1970 he lost. Unruh, a big man, had dieted, had polished his verbal delivery, but he was still unable to project himself on television successfully. Despite his manifest ability, the nickname "Big Daddy" stuck. "He cannot accomplish image-making," said Salzman.

In terms of simple honesty, freedom from illegality, and general efficiency, local government within California probably does reach high standards. Scandals like that surrounding "Mr. San Diego"—the banker C. Arnholt Smith who was the driving force in San Diego's rapid 1960s expansion and whose bank ultimately failed to the tune of $200 million—such scandals are the exception in recent California history.

Sacramento, too, is reputed to be the most efficient state government in the country. Certainly it is immensely professional and expert, with legislators backed by personal and committee staffs on a scale not found in other states.

In other words, the operation of publicity principles and populist politics has not necessarily meant in California that administration, local or state, is inherently worse. On the contrary; the workings of the huge University of California are often hailed as an example of disinterested and efficient administration. Yet at various key points the need for money for campaigns has a potentially corrupting effect.

While "big league" publicity does not touch the 80 assembly

or 40 senate members, media publicity is very important for
most of them. One example is the sheer volume of new proposed legislation. In March 1979, only three months into the
new legislative session, some 1300 bills had already been introduced into the assembly and 900 into the senate.* Much of this
is anxious legislators introducing rhetorical statements in the
form of bills in order to capitalize on the advantages of incum-
bency and to score publicity points with electors back home.

The biggest job in the California legislature—and "second
most powerful job in Sacramento"—has been speaker of the
assembly. The recent potency of this job dates back to Jesse
Unruh, who was speaker from 1961 to 1968. Leo McCarthy
consolidated its importance in the 1970s. Nobody can object to
the elected leader of an elected legislature having power. But
there are some senses in which the "imperial speakership" of
Sacramento came in to fill a vacuum left by the demise of the
imperial lobbyist, Samish, in 1949. The assembly speakership
under Unruh, acquired key powers over committee assign-
ments, staffs, and the like. However, equally significant the
speakership acquired power as a focal point through which favors could be done for lobbyists in return for election finance.
This not only gave the speaker clout with the lobbyists—he
could deliver the votes of the majority party in the assembly—
but it gave the speaker leverage with the assembly members
because he could decide to which of them he would channel
the election finance. And in turn this election finance power
was significant to assembly members who operated under California conditions of large constituencies, weak party loyalty,
and expensive media-oriented elections.

Many assembly races are professionally managed (although
this was another service Leo McCarthy could supply direct).
The more general point is that, under prevailing California
conditions of numerous noisy campaigns, almost all candidates
at election time need to communicate aggressively with their
local electorate. This may be by way of radio advertising, or it
may mean billboards and direct mail. But it is expensive and
leaves all legislators permanently obsessed with publicity in
general and money for publicity in particular.

*During the 1979–80 session 1,445 bills passed the legislature.

Media obsessions seem to permeate Sacramento politics in an even more fundamental way. California politicians operate in an environment of very aggressive single-issue campaigning. It is widely believed that under these conditions negative campaigns are more effective ("if you've got enough money you can't pass any proposition but you can stop any proposition from being passed"). Politicians go in fear of the single key mistake—such as a vote in favor of an unpopular piece of major legislation—which can be made the basis of a negative campaign at the next election.

Doug Kriegel, the only Sacramento-based correspondent of a Los Angeles television station (KNBC), put it to us this way (in March 1979) in explanation of why most of the "liberals" in the Democratic-controlled assembly had recently voted against school busing: "Sacramento is a fast track. One mistake—like an unpopular vote on busing—can be costly. They've been wearing those suits for years, trying to get themselves here. The fear index is strong."

Unruh might have fared better in a newspaper-dominated age, but (in Los Angeles) the end of almost unchallenged newspaper political power can be symbolically dated to 1960. That was the year one of California's most tireless candidates for public office, Samuel W. Yorty, ran for mayor of Los Angeles against the incumbent Norrie Poulson. Poulson enjoyed the support of all the metropolitan papers, especially the *Los Angeles Times,* which was an old enemy of Yorty's. Yorty turned to television, and cheap television at that—the daytime audience of housewives. Yorty found a "natural" issue: trash collection. He won the race, and the election represented one of the first triumphs of television publicity over the political coverage of the metropolitan dailies. One television man said of the outcome of the campaign, "that was the day we draped the *Times* building in black crepe."

Yorty had in previous campaigns made a thing of his black moustache. In 1960 he shaved it off. On television, he had been advised, he looked too much like a Mexican bandit. Without it, he was a sympathetic personality. As mayor he ran his own television show, a Los Angeles boosters' program which kept him nicely in the public eye until events such as those in

Watts in 1965 made Sam Yorty known nationally. A Yorty television show ran on local Los Angeles television for years, even surviving his defeat by Tom Bradley in 1973 for the mayor's job. It was only taken off (due to slipping ratings) in 1980.

Hollywood in Politics

Active Hollywood involvement in politics began in 1934. The years 1934–66 saw the attachment of celebrities to national political campaigns. Since then, changing election finance laws have made performers a valuable addition to any politician's bandwagon. Certain political causes now benefit disproportionately from celebrity interest. The campaign against nuclear energy is one: a string of stars from Jane Fonda to Joni Mitchell, Linda Ronstadt, Graham Nash, Bonnie Raitt, and other laid-back southern California popular musicians have been on the anti-nuclear wagon for some time. And in 1978 some 40 to 50 percent of the financial support for the campaign against the initiative to restrict homosexual teachers in the state of California came from Hollywood. Music managers Jerry Weintraub and Irving Azoff have given "substantial sums" to Senator Alan Cranston, a Democrat. Leading television entrepreneur Norman Lear, one of Hollywood's most vocal advocates in the 1970s of more adult television, has given vocal and financial support to a variety of national and California Democratic politicians. "I've always felt I was a citizen first," he is quoted as saying, "even when people asked what someone in our business could know about politics. The only difference now is that politicians take my phone calls."[5]

And there is the Fonda phenomenon. Jane Fonda, daughter of Henry, has emerged from a notably successful film career as a political operator of great resourcefulness and some originality. Together with her husband, former student agitator Tom Hayden, she is the only celebrity to have a political organization built around her—the Campaign for Economic Democracy. CED is also derived from Hayden's remarkably strong challenge in the 1976 U.S. Senate Democratic primary

5. Michele Willens, "The Hollywood-Washington Connection," *California Journal,* August 1979.

against the incumbent, John Tunney. Taking much of its ideology from the leftovers of 1960's radicalism, the campaign is not all pie-in-the-sky—it has had success in moves to stabilize rents in the wake of Proposition 13 in such communities as Santa Monica where Jane and Tom live.[6] Fonda is strong on solar and nuclear power issues: she has a habit in speechmaking of comparing the "facts" of her movie *The China Syndrome* with the "fictions" of government pronouncements on the subject.

Hayden-Fonda have been courted by Jerry Brown. He made a political blunder of the first order by appointing Fonda to the state arts commission, an appointment the state's legislators did not like one bit. They reprocessed Fonda's pronouncements on the Vietnam War as evidence of her unfitness: she was not confirmed. Hayden has been luckier: he sits on the state solar energy and border commissions.

Hollywood has given Californian politics three kinds of gifts: former actors turned politicians; media skills to be put to use in politics; and a version of celebrity as a universal quality to be transferred between screen and hustings at will.

One of the campaign consultants we talked to was Sandy Weiner, based in San Francisco. We caught up with him in the middle of the special election for the U.S. House of Representatives called to replace Congressman Leo Ryan, killed in pursuit of the People's Temple religious cult in Guyana with a posse of mediamen surrounding him. Earlier, Weiner had paused to remember an episode in his career as media manipulator:

> A semi-retired but still handsome silver-haired movie actor and I sat up one night discussing the premise that if charisma was the most potent factor in winning elections, then why shouldn't a handsome goodguy movie star with twinkling eyes be the epitome of all that was happening? We decided the idea was worth pursuing.
> Starting with a campaign war chest of $1,000, and despite the derision of other politicians in California, a

6. Joel Kotkin, "Tom Hayden's Manifest Destiny," *Esquire,* May 1980.

year later George Murphy became a United States senator.[7]

George Murphy was no mere actor; he was an accomplished song-and-dance man once touted by Louella Parsons—some accolade this—as the successor to Bing Crosby when Murphy arrived in Hollywood after a Broadway career in the 1930s. It was Louis B. Mayer, that prominent Republican, who first saw Murphy's political potential. Mayer dispatched Murphy as an "ambassador of goodwill" to luncheons of B'nai B'rith and Knights of Columbus to dispel the idea that the movies were crawling with Communists. Murphy even won a special Academy Award for these public relations activities—in 1940, twenty-four years before his election to the U.S. Senate.

In one of his well-loved pictures, *Little Miss Broadway* (1938), Murphy's co-star was the moppet heroine Shirley Temple. Later she, too, married to a California businessman, exchanged the sound stage for the political platform. In 1967 she was the media favorite to win the primary for a special election from San Mateo, then California's 11th Congressional District; but the election was won by Paul McCloskey—possibly because Black's campaign, orchestrated by Whitaker and Baxter, was too low key. Shirley Temple Black had in fact already put in several years' hard toil in the vineyards of Californian state Republicanism and has since shown her ability in public office. Make no mistake, Temple and Murphy did not walk ready-made into politics, they probably did more than their fair share of benefits, dinners, and gladhanding. Name and reputation helped.

George Murphy recounts in his appropriately titled autobiography *"Say . . . didn't you used to be George Murphy?"* how he put knowledge gained in the pictures to use in politics; for a Senate speech, he tells us, on the subject of migrant labor, much of his apparently detailed knowledge of braceros came from filming *Border Incident* (1949) with Ricardo Montalban for MGM. George Murphy did not consider that the financial assistance he received from his former employers at Technicolor

7. Elizabeth Heighton and Don Cunningham, *Advertising in the Broadcast Media*, Belmont, Ca., 1976, p. 326.

Corporation, while in the U. S. Senate, amounted to the purchase of political favor. The electors did, though they continued to like actors. Or rather celebrities: Murphy's replacement in the Senate in 1970 was John Tunney, born into the celebrity of his father, Gene Tunney, the victor in the boxing ring over Jack Dempsey—an early example of the sportsman lionized by movie stars. Douglas Fairbanks made the elder Tunney a regular and welcome guest at Pickfair. Tunney, Jr. (who still appears regularly on KABC TV and performs like an indifferent actor playing J. F. Kennedy) had six not very distinguished years in the Senate. One high point came in 1972 when he previewed "his" film *The Candidate* (in which "he" was played by Robert Redford). Intended as an exposé of the slick media-based techniques on which political success was now built, the film turned into a celebration: Tunney's former speechwriter Jerry Larner wrote the screenplay; his campaign manager Nelson Rising was the movie's associate producer; bit parts were played by colleagues of Tunney's and sundry California real-life politicians.

California politics are not unique in their intimacy with the celebrity principle. In 1978 the electors of New Jersey sent a basketball star to the U.S. Senate; Virginia deployed the husband of that national institution, Elizabeth Taylor. In the state of Ohio a former spaceman made the political grade by trading one form of elevated celebrity for another. Jack Kemp of New York is, however, the recent politician who best illustrates that media politics are both essentially California and also literally transferable from the Southwest to the Northeast. Before Jack Kemp was elected to Congress in 1970 from an Erie County, N.Y., district he had been a superstar quarterback for the San Diego Chargers and the Buffalo Bills; he had acquired political experience both in entertainment trade unionism (co-founder and president of the AFL Players Association, 1965–70) and in public relations (for a leading Buffalo bank); like Ronald Reagan, Kemp had been a radio commentator. In fact he worked for Reagan himself as special assistant to the governor.

It is the ease of transfer (or crossover in Hollywood parlance) that singles out the California experience. California politicians have become media stars as readily as its screen stars have become politicians. To take but one example: observers in Washington, D.C., were startled when the Representative from California's 27th Congressional District gallantly offered himself as a substitute hostage during the Hanafi muslim siege in Washington in March 1977 (since neither he nor his district had any connection with this brand of black Islam). The puzzlement soon lifted. The 27th District includes much of the swinging west side of Los Angeles, and in 1976 Congressman Bob Dornan, formerly a local TV talk show host on KTLA, had been the victor—"in the highest spending house campaign in history" at that time. Perhaps the lure of the cameras and the possibility of stardom as a hostage on national television had been too great a temptation.

In the Democratic primaries held in June 1980 there was a minor contretemps in one of the Los Angeles state assembly districts. Incumbent Representative Mike Roos went before a judge to demand free television time. His challenger had an unfair advantage, Roos claimed: the challenger (who later withdrew) was George Takei, otherwise known as Mr Sulu, gallant first officer of *Star Trek*'s Starship Enterprise.

Brown and Curb

In Jerry Brown, we seem to have the archetypal California politician—at least enough of one to convince the cartoonists and columnists. The first element in Brown's success was simply that his "name recognition"—as the son of a popular two-term governor—was high. Second, like the movie star's son who has been observing his father's moves all along, Brown had a very highly developed sense of how to publicize himself. Brown has gained financially by his attractiveness to the new Hollywood—especially popular music. His 1978 campaign for governor benefited from concert takings at events featuring pro-Brown groups. Yet Gray Davis, Brown's campaign manager, admitted that the music fans were not necessarily enamored of Governor Brown's existentialism or his mode of governing the state. "People go to one of our concerts," said Davis, "basically to see the Eagles perform. Frankly we'd have trouble getting one-fifth of the people there just to see Jerry."

Brown of course made his own Hollywood connection, without intermediaries: through Linda Ronstadt, a winsome former country singer who has successfully made the transition into a generic popular musician. An almost perfect example of California syncretism, she has borrowed musically from every source. With a home in Malibu, a former boyfriend in the Eagles, and the governor of the state of California at her elbow, she has never lacked for useful publicity. A much-publicized trip to Africa with Jerry Brown, shortly before the start of the 1980 Presidential primaries gave her celebrity another boost: for several weeks that useful index of public attention, the Johnny Carson show, was not complete without some reference to the couple's peregrinations.

Not that Governor Brown depended for his fame on the prospect of a rock singer as first lady. Early in his first term as governor he could have walked into any California radio or television station any time of the day or night and been given air time. This needs some explaining. There is evidence that Brown's victories in statewide contests have had a lot more to do with the weakness of his opponents than his own attractiveness as a candidate: who remembers his opponent in the gubernatorial race in 1974, for example (Houston Flournoy)? Evelle Younger (an extremely wooden attorney general of California) his challenger in 1978, took a holiday in the Hawaiian Islands after the primaries and allowed Brown to grab enormous media attention for his dramatic conversion to the tax-cutting concept of Proposition 13. By the time Younger was back from his vacation, Brown had eaten and digested his own words and was in splendid media form for the main election. Following a decades long California tradition, Brown has been surrounded by media-conscious aides. One, Thomas Quinn, ought to be given much of the credit for Brown's successful projection. Quinn seems to have an especially acute understanding of the publicity possibilities of radio. Quinn is now chairman of the major local news agency in Los Angeles County, City News: his father occupied the position before him. His formative years were spent writing press releases which he often had the pleasure of hearing read back to him over local Los Angeles radio stations as "the news."

"I think he is one of the best I've seen on television. He's got a good poker face . . . When you're talking to him directly he'll show annoyance, but not on TV. He must have watched all my mistakes." This is Brown senior discussing Brown junior with Orville Schell, one of Jerry's biographers. Another biographer takes this preoccupation with media imagery further. "On television Jerry is an expert at make-up and how to sit and move . . . He can be aloof and detached until the red light on the television camera shows and then he instantly turns on." Thus the governor's celebrated predilection for "buzz words"— a product according to his former press secretary Elizabeth Coleman of an intense fascination with what newsmen and reporters need to make a story go. Orville Schell has a conversation with Brown about the media. Brown is skeptical of the notion of "image"; rather the media "have decided" that people want personalities and not issues. The basis of the media is selling, says Brown.

And Amen to that from Mike Curb, Brown's Republican deputy, elected at age thirty-three. Curb is another Hollywood import into California politics, one of the first to make the move from the record business, a new arrival in the Beverly Hills community. Feet on the desk in his Sacramento office, Mike Curb told us: "Being a Republican, I think I was the first Republican this century in California to carry the 18–34 vote. I think the young people in California relate to the music industry. They've grown up with it, they relate to the artists and many of them relate specifically to some of my artists. One of my top artists [in our interview Curb discussed "my artists" in the present tense, despite his claim not to have been engaged in the music business since elected lieutenant-governor six months earlier] is Frankie Vallee and the Four Seasons; right in the middle of the 1978 campaign Frankie had *Grease*. Although *Grease* appeared on the Robert Stigwood label, the *Grease* single appeared in our album, our Warner/Curb album. We also in the middle of the campaign had the biggest selling record in the history of the record business *You Light Up My Life* by Debbie Boone. . . ."

Beneath the hyperbole is a straight selling pitch; during the campaign all those millions of discs were spinning round with the name of Curb on them. Curb used to be president of MGM Records before that casino/hotel company cut its losses in the music business and sold out to the conglomerate Polygram. Curb has a charming young wife and a house in the hills behind Los Angeles—a clean-cut Christian-image politician who parlayed his reputation as a whizz-kid in records into standing in the state Republican party (not least by organizing the musical entertainments in 1973 at President Richard M. Nixon's second inaugural). His only (but very Hollywoodesque) blemish has to do with his business practices in the past: they may have been common in the record industry, but they smell.[8] His opponent in the 1978 election Mervyn Dymally put it brutally: "The record industry is a whole rip-off industry. A young kid comes and gives his talent. The middleman, who Curb is, makes all the money. Here's a punk kid (Curb) who's just recruited and is pouring money into this race as if it were going out of style. Sure it galls ya. I mean, that's the nature of Californian politics."[9] The Republican attorney-general of California was impelled to investigate Curb's business past during 1979. A tipster claimed that he had once given Curb a suitcase full of money at a Los Angeles restaurant in exchange for unspecified favors. But Curb was pronounced clean in November 1979. And Dymally, the black politician who made the original charges, himself fell under scrutiny: his stake in a Los Angeles laundromat operation had been bought with suspicious money, and some of that had bought him into the race for lieutenant-governor (in which Dymally spent some $800,000 to Curb's $1.5 million).

Ronald Reagan

Ronald Reagan will go down in the history books as the consummate California politician, launched on his career by his reputation as a movie actor. (His detractors would add that you don't even have to be a particularly good actor. Before World War II, he won the support of Hedda Hopper as a leading

8. Maureen Orth and Bruce Henderson, "The Flip Side of Mike Curb's Career," *New West,* November 6, 1978.
9. *Los Angeles Times,* November 7, 1978.

man of the future.) Reagan was a fair to moderate actor, certainly no worse than scores of other junior leading men at the
time. He was, however, a victim of the studio system, leaving it
for war service just at the point in his career when he should
have been attracting wider attention and better roles. By 1945
he had missed several steps in the would-be star's upward pro-
gression. Reagan was also badly advised, as he himself has re-
counted: "Back in '36, we used to make three or four movies a
year and we loved it. But in 1940 the wartime emergency sur-
tax went up to 96 percent at the top of the scale and my agent
told me 'You can't make more than one movie a year.' So what
happened is that instead of working for the whole year, we sat
around the Brown Derby looking for oil deals." [10] Reagan was
a liberal Democrat at the time and did not become an ardent
tax-reformer till twenty years later. He was, perhaps partly because of his less than starry post-1945 career in movies, an enthusiastic and adroit labor unionist, with a talent for overall
strategy and for holding the Screen Actors' Guild together,
rather than for the details of negotiations. It was as the president of SAG (1947–54 and 1959–60) that Reagan first demonstrated his chairmanly political style.

Reagan's conversion from labor unionist and F.D.R. liberal,
which he admits to being prior to 1940, into a right-wing en-
thusiast was essentially private. When he emerged during the
1950s as an itinerant spokesman and gladhander for General
Electric, his right wing views—his new views—were jelling. And
when he achieved a second burst of stardom as host of the TV
adventure series *Death Valley Days* his views were considered
fairly far out, even by the standards of the decidedly illiberal
Borax Mining Company, the Californian corporation sponsor-
ing the show (the company made its money excavating borax
on the great salt flats of Death Valley, China Lake and the California deserts). Thereafter Reagan, the ranch owner, never
strayed far from the state's major power blocs: his co-sponsor
of the Republican state campaign on behalf of Senator Barry
Goldwater in 1964 was the president of the state's largest citrus
marketing organization. But for all his right-wing fervor, Rea-

10. *Washington Post,* March 23, 1980.

gan was one of the best governors the state's bureaucrats in
Sacramento had known to date. Eisenhower-like, he was content to let an efficient machine run itself. His appointments,
pro-business, generally had integrity; his 1970–72 welfare reforms worked. Almost Reagan's first move in office was to step
up the California state income tax which, in a booming economy, piled up the revenue surplus that lasted till after Proposition 13 passed.

By then its was obvious that a successful campaign had two
ingredients: television and radio plus professional campaign
management. Reagan's camp chose the then highly successful
firm of Spencer-Roberts, a latter-day successor to Whitaker and
Baxter. Middle-income households, where the voters were,
watched most television; A. C. Nielsen affirmed it. So television
was where Ronald Reagan spent his dollars. After the successful campaign, Governor Reagan continued to use television for
the fresh presentation, at intervals of a few weeks, of dramatic
new initiatives. Reagan excelled on the media—he had had
plenty of experience—whereas his opponent of 1966, Edmund
G. "Pat" Brown, was stolid.

Hollywood produces politicians. But just as Ronald Reagan
was not the first actor to become a major California politician,
so also non-actor California politicians have had actors' qualities. Richard Nixon for one.

Nixon as California Politician and Television Performer

Richard Nixon was heavily marked by California life and politics, especially media politics. Television had already brought
fame to, for example, Senator Estes Kefauver. But it was Nixon
who in his famous "Checkers" speech in 1952 demonstrated
the full possibilities of political salvation via television.

Nixon was shaped by life before 1940 in Whittier, a small
town outside Los Angeles. He was always a great believer in
California myths and institutions. He matured as his home
town was engulfed by the march of the Los Angeles suburbs
into Orange County. Later as a young Whittier lawyer, Nixon
participated in the California real estate booms.

Nixon always had a fascination for Hollywood, only twenty-five miles away; it was where you went on Saturday nights in the late 1930s. Nixon was from his schooldays a performer. He was an accomplished debater; in the navy he made substantial sums (which helped to finance his first election) as a poker-player; and, at least until age twenty-seven, he was an enthusiastic and successful amateur actor. Several biographies of Nixon stress his weak sense of his own identity—a common trait in actors. Moreover, Nixon married an actress—Pat Nixon played small parts in two Hollywood films—and Nixon's highly revealing book *My Six Crises* shows that again and again he sees politics in terms of playing roles. He also regards himself as a judge of others' performances. He initially made his name by suspecting that Alger Hiss's performance was not authentic. In his famous U.S. Senate race of 1950 he managed to upstage Helen Gahagan Douglas, the first Hollywood performer to hold national office.

Nixon had the qualities of role-playing and projection which have been common to most California politicians who have won state-wide office, the qualities needed to appeal to the electorate of a large state with weak parties. Nixon was helped enormously in 1950 by being a favorite protégé of the *Los Angeles Times*, but from the very start of his political career he was a master of vivid imagery. He entered politics by answering a newspaper advertisement and used his sense of the dramatic to appear (in late 1945) in naval officer's uniform.

There is certainly a California angle to the crisis which Nixon calls "the fund" but which everyone else refers to as the "Checkers speech"—in the final act of the melodrama Nixon's bravura television performance contains a reference to the family pet dog Checkers. The address delivered in Los Angeles on September 23, 1952, to a national television and radio audience produced an extraordinary positive public response, and left Eisenhower no option but to retain Nixon as his running mate. The later account of "the fund" by Nixon is a powerful piece of dramatic writing—even though he diplomatically omits to mention delicate details, such as that he was deliberately pressing not only Stevenson but also Eisenhower to reveal all personal financial details. We see Nixon on a whistle-stop speaking tour around California as the crisis builds, and we observe him trying out his response on live audiences. We sense Nixon's fear and hatred of the eastern Republican high command around Eisenhower, who—Nixon realizes full well—want to drop this embarrassing West Coast hick. The speech itself has a Hollywood aura about it. It is made in Hollywood. Nixon—initially suffers from intense debilitating stage fright and wants to withdraw as he is leaving his hotel; his entourage—notably his actress wife Pat and go-for-the-jugular political consultant Murray Chotiner—almost drag him to the studio. Once he is speaking without notes—having had time to memorize the speech only in part—Nixon's nerves disappear, and he delivers the speech in true bravura style. Actor-like, he is disappointed because at the end he fluffs the final line. The first person to congratulate him is the make-up man, who with Hollywood professionalism knows a riveting performance when he sees one. In the last reel the thirty-nine-year-old star has upstaged everyone—both Stevenson and Ike, the entire Republican eastern establishment, and the press.

It has been pointed out that Nixon deliberately let the crisis get worse and worse—partly perhaps because the friendly Republican press of California had given him no experience of newspaper attacks (the story which initiated the fund "scandal" appeared in the *New York Post,* written by a Hollywood reporter named Leo Katcher.). But Nixon had become involved with the fund only because of a problem to any U.S. Senator from California; "the fund" had been created from donations whose purpose was to allow Nixon to send regular mailings to supporters and financial contributors throughout California. Nixon needed the fund problem because of distance (within the state and between West Coast and East Coast) and the California politician's instinct for "keeping in touch" with his backers. "Checkers" is an odd episode in a political career in which later, Nixon seemed unable to use television effectively (witness the controversy over the 1960 Presidential debates with John Kennedy).

California of course has no monopoly on "posers" for office; nor on media campaign consultants. The styles and apparatus of modern media politics had an initial run in the far West. We may expect California to be in the vanguard of development of the political use of media and money—such as the current trend to direct-mail campaigns which simultaneously solicit votes and money with which to finance further publicity.

9
California:
State of the Media

Simple facts of time and distance conspire to make California a state of odd ball news. In the United States, news traditionally travels east to west; California is three hours behind New York, making the appearance of "hard" news from California in major media unlikely.

For example, when it is noon in Washington and New York much of what will appear on the network television news has already happened, but in California it is still only 9 a.m. The time zones make it almost impossible for anyone in the East ever to read the *Los Angeles Times* and find out whether or not it is better than the *Washington Post*. (In fact, the *Los Angeles Times* tries to beat the time zone penalty by flying and then hand-delivering a small number of copies in a few key buildings in the East.)

One main consequence of time zones is that the national news media tend to ignore California as a source of hard news but rely on it for colorful or offbeat items. Hence the state's oddball reputation. Other states have mass killings, mud slides, forest fires, zany religions, improbable politicians, and outlandish behavior, but the American public has been taught by the news media that bizarre happenings are especially likely to come from California. Maybe America needs California as a sort of safety valve, the symbolic location of national libido; the media oblige. Journalists in California report that stories they file are changed in the East. From deep in the third paragraph key "oddball" words are pulled up front: such words as Patty Hearst, fashion, cult, disaster, sex, and murder. Reeve Hennion, UPI's western regional editor, confirmed this.

> The time difference hurts us, but not in the sense that less space is devoted to it. California news gets tremendous play (in the East)—only later. Nuts, fruitcakes, of the world in California . . . this is the typical New York deskman's view.
>
> Every once in a while we have a story we think is significant, and we can convince New York. But there is general expectation that California will produce screwball happenings.

Thus stories about earthquakes or new and bizarre lifestyles: the gatekeepers of news-agency news consider California a great center for social trends. And the disciplines of news-gathering reinforce this.

Yet maybe the deskmen have a point. Asked to name the major headline stories that had gone across his desk in the late 1970s, Martin Thompson, AP's bureau chief in San Francisco, produced a hair-raising list. It began with the abduction of Patty Hearst, the country's first political kidnapping and an event that, Thompson remarked, generated the most copy in San Francisco since Korean War material was routed through the city. He went on: the George Jackson shootout at Marin County court-house; mass murders in Yuba City; the "Zebra" killings; the assassination of Mayor George Moscone and Supervisor Harvey Milk; the kidnapping of an entire busload of children at Chowchilla; the "Zodiac" killer, and assassination attempts on President Gerald Ford both in Sacramento and in San Francisco. (And this list, of course, was only a *northern* California catalog of facts fitting stereotypes.)

Thus California is in an obvious sense a media source for the rest of America. So, it must inevitably be said, is New York;

indeed the list of New York's recent headline-catching stories is also chilling. New York, albeit to a lesser extent than California, produces the fare of network television; its streets serve as movie backdrops; its theaters on Broadway are still the original sources of some Hollywood shows. Arguing as we do that California is a "state of the media" in no way exhausts the significance in American mass media of New York; in fact, the Beverly Hills occupational community has roots historical and personal there, and east-west movement is routine. Broadway has been dependent since the 1920s on Hollywood finance and in recent years has increasingly attracted film and TV stars whose careers in Hollywood are faltering. The media in America are strung out along a New York-California axis. The only way fully to comprehend the American entertainment industry is to be based in both Hollywood and New York—a truth well understood by *Variety,* with its sober weekly New York main edition and its more glossy Hollywood *Daily Variety.*

New York and California have much in common; both are centers of production for the rest of America, or "flyoverland." They are also paraded as cultural opposites. Woody Allen's film *Annie Hall* (1977) amusingly presents all the prejudices of the easterner confronting the West. Los Angeles has sunshine and libido, is laid back and shallow; New York has snow, ego, tension, and depth. The only cultural advantage of life in California is being able to make a right turn on a red light. New York represents serious authority (money, news, advertising, culture), while California represents fantasy and escapism (the television series, films and records on which the public spends such an incredible number of hours per week). The stereotypes have only limited value, but in both centers of media production there is without doubt a constant dialog about making material acceptable to and comprehensible by a national audience, while the program-makers live in a local community and share its reflexes. Neither Manhattan nor Malibu is exactly typically American.

The local element in California media is at once obvious, yet difficult to tease out. Ronald Reagan, campaigning in Los Angeles in 1966, found himself addressing a meeting of the Huntington Park Republican women: "I've a warm spot in my heart for Huntington Park," he told them. "My first picture for Warner's had its sneak preview in Huntington Park in 1937."

The definition of all-American taste by means of California still goes on. On Sunset Boulevard in Los Angeles is a 400-seat theater that serves as a "preview house." Operated by ASI Market Research, it is used by ABC and NBC to test pilot television programs. Invitations are passed out in local shopping malls. There are dials on the seats to indicate approval (the dials are pre-set on a standard scale determined for each audience by their response to a Mr. Magoo cartoon shown to them first). Note that California is not unique here: CBS runs its own testing facility on similar lines in New York.

But does the existence of a local element in programing mean that California values are superimposed? Frank Mankiewicz, now head of National Public Radio but in 1972 manager of George McGovern's Presidential campaign, said yes. Recalling his thirty-seven years as a California resident, he told us: "The America of commercials on television is Californian." He listed their values: "miscegenation, bright clothes, eternally youthful women, Lite beer with gusto . . . that's the Californian view."

Mankiewicz had a point; he was talking about California values being hedonistic, and about the abandonment, in California's media products, of discrimination, geographical, cultural, and (to an extent) racial. The association of California and libido is an old one. "Nothing epitomized the hedonism of the United States better than the state of California," lamented Daniel Bell,[1] worried that fun morality and sex would dissolve the ties binding American society together in the 1970s. Certainly, the western region's own myth emphasizes California's brightness, its sunny disposition, its facilities for the good life (which is not far from the truth, for the affluent majority). Odd scraps of data—such as a 1979 *Los Angeles Times* sample survey—suggest that southern Californians think they are happier—at least compared with New Yorkers. However, the "lotus-land" reputation of California—mentioned in the

1. Bell's main authority for this, quoted in his book, is a cover story from *Time* magazine, "California: A State of Excitement." Daniel Bell, *The Cultural Contradictions of Capitalism*, London, 1979, pp. 70–71.

Time magazine article from which Daniel Bell quotes—is fairly mythical. And from year-round observation of the beach at La Jolla Shores—one of the most lotus-land-like spots in California—we can report that most Californians visit beaches, if at all, only on weekends. In other words, if entertainment programing from California presents a "picture of the world," it is generally likely to be a falsely leisured and a falsely happy one. By the phrase "abandonment of discrimination," we mean nothing pejorative. Rather, that a characteristic of California has always been the ease with which the most apparently incongruous styles of life, dress, architecture, and decoration can be married beneath the state's benign skies. Los Angeles speech pathologists, who enjoy a good living, say that most people living there want a non-regional accent. Nasal New York tones are disliked. Californians want to sound "like they come from nowhere." In parallel in the Californian media there is an ease of transfer. The local desert masquerades as the Sahara; strip cartoons turn into films, and novels into TV pilots; the latest series of bizarre California murders becomes the pilot show for a possible TV series.

In this sense California culture is syncretic. There are no barriers to reinterpretation, to translation. *Daily Variety* put the same point in a discussion of television, calling it "a medium which lives by spinoffs of series, which are variations of that original skein, which in many cases wasn't original."[2] California has become, culturally speaking, the best possible locale for the mass entertainment industries. California values other qualities, and reflects them in the local component of the media programing. Mobility is one. The climate suits arduous action, and movement is the be-all and end-all of a culture based on the automobile. Local news on KABC is fast-paced and action-packed; so is each episode of *CHiPs*. Another quality is the appreciation of celebrity for its own sake. But in California perhaps proximity to Hollywood made celebrity even more valued, and spread it to every walk of life. "Let's face it," said gubernatorial aide Gary Davis, "people are more into the lives, habits and political preferences of today's celebrities. I mean, it

2. *Daily Variety*, October 4, 1979.

might sound ridiculous, but people really care who is Suzanne Sommers's favorite Governor."[3] Who is, of course, Davis's boss, Jerry Brown. Association with celebrity, as we saw in Chapter 2, often substitutes for substance in Californian programing. There is a danger of mistaking Beverly Hills and Hollywood for the immensely diverse state of California. Similarly Hollywood is often discussed completely sundered from its Californian setting. Hollywood, meaning the diversified media occupational community of Los Angeles, is anchored in California by its dependence on Sierra water; in the historical context of Los Angeles civic and labor policies; and in the symbolical sense that Hollywood's backlot, used by film-makers and talk show hosts alike, is as wide as the state—and extends beyond to Las Vegas, Honolulu, and Acapulco.

The local connection has obtruded on the immaculate history of film at many points. To take only one example: Hedda Hopper, doyenne of the columnists, went on radio to tell the world about the stars, courtesy of the state of California's largest citrus marketing organization—Sunkist.

Hollywood and Sacramento are allied by the community's gifts to politics. Jeff Wald, husband and manager of singer Helen Reddy, has been a big contributor to Governor Jerry Brown's campaigns. In Wald's opinion, Brown returns the compliment: "Brown," he told reporters, "knows how to use the media. Part of his relationship with the entertainment community comes from a common understanding about the media. They are stars and Jerry Brown is a star."[4]

Sacramento—Media Capital

California is, like New York, in the vanguard of other states in having built up a body of influential media case law as well as extensive statewide media regulations. Take the music business. New York and California are the states in which most recording contracts are entered into.[5] California statute law limits the

---

3. Quoted in *San Francisco Chronicle*, April 4, 1979.
4. *San Francisco Chronicle* April 4, 1979.
5. S. Shemel and M. Wilson Krasilovsky, *This Business of Music*, New York, 1977, p. 5.

length of personal service contracts and specifies, uniquely, the respective jobs of personal managers and agents (New York state law contents itself by regulating theatrical employment agencies). The state's anti-piracy laws on unauthorized reproduction of music recordings are tougher than elsewhere. It was a California lower court that preceded the finding in federal law that film rights descended to heirs: the widow of Bela Lugosi, the movie actor, had sued Universal Pictures over the licensing rights in the character of Count Dracula. California law is broadly accommodating to media interests, but not always. In 1979 the state legislature passed a cable television bill which has implications for other states. Instead of fragmented city-by-city regulation, the California law allows cable companies to opt for state regulation. This presents them with a trade-off; contributions to a public-access fund in exchange for freedom to raise rates.

More media legislation can be expected from Sacramento in the future. The Hispanic thrust in California politics is unlikely—in the long run—to ignore the legislative leverage Sacramento potentially has over Beverly Hills. California may well lead the country in state media legislation.

In a similar way, California's Congressional delegation has been involved in detail in federal media matters. And interest has not been confined to congressmen like Henry Waxman, from a district containing part of Hollywood, who are direct spokespeople for the media community. Waxman, in 1980, attempted to introduce legislation that would have excused from federal equal-time provision entertainment performances by "bona-fide" actors and celebrities running for political office. Media issues have interested Barry Goldwater, Jr., Congressman from a district to the northwest of Los Angeles and—despite his and his father's anti-labor union philosophy—he has been an active worker for Hollywood trade unions as well as other entertainment industry interests. California's most active media legislator in the late 1970s was Congressman Lionel Van Deerlin (from a Democratic district in San Diego), chairman of the House communications sub-committee. Van Deerlin's positions refuted any simple idea that California politicians merely reflect local interests: the broadcasting networks were never happy with Van Deerlin's attempt to rewrite the whole basis of federal media law by scrapping the 1934 Communication Act. Yet Van Deerlin—former Tijuana broadcaster and experienced San Diego journalist—certainly had a California media perspective. (Ironically Van Deerlin lost his "safe" seat in 1980. His Republican opponent combined personal campaigning with a late media blitz.)

Van Deerlin's bill was a vision of a free market in broadcasting: releasing the airways to a host of new, mostly commercial and competing voices. It works in Los Angeles radio, so why not nationally? Van Deerlin proposed wide deregulation of television and radio. The vision, his critics said, was that of a Californian blind to the concentration of power in the hands of media conglomerates to which market forces meant only the working of a de facto cartel. Some might say also that Van Deerlin's vision of largely deregulated media reflects—in a curious echo of Governor Hiram Johnson's political reforms—an ex-journalist's suspicion of "bureaucracy" (the FCC).

While Van Deerlin's failure to sell his package to his fellow Democrats in the House was in a sense a failure, another interpretation is that the episode is indicative of things to come. It illustrates the importance of media legislation in Washington, the increasing centrality of Washington for the media.

Media Made in California

Our contention in this book has been that American media can be better understood by examining their California component. This would be advisable, naturally, if California were merely a populous state with 23 million-plus people; but the circumstances of California history and the location of the entertainment-producing industries make it even more so. And California's diversity allows us to play both sides of the street and appraise the state's media as providing at once typical and special cases of American problems.

California displays, for example, two problems of competence in the coverage by all American media of public institutions. Mainstream television finds politics a difficult subject, except where it can be personalized. Or, to put it in the hackneyed yet perceptive words of Governor Jerry Brown, "the logic of the media requires an escalation in the incongruity, in the excitement, in the fascination, to constantly overcome the tedium and the boredom that politics really is."[6]

The networks, with their own traditions and machinery of national newsgathering, are relied upon for nearly all television news from the centers of American life outside the state. Meanwhile, City Hall is easy to reach, so "Eyewitness News" teams can take it in as part of the daily roster of stories. But "middle-distance" news is missed. In California, the problem—in both San Francisco and Los Angeles—is news from a middle-distance place that happens to be the state capital, Sacramento. Newspapers perform better on middle-distance news, but those in California—typically—are content to leave vast tracts of Californian America overcovered. To rely on the seven-man AP bureau in Sacramento—as many Californian dailies to a large extent do—means that adequate coverage of governmental agencies must go by default. Some major specialized areas of state government get little coverage, and opinionated or investigative journalism is also missing. Sacramento is the best single location for analyzing the political economy of California. Federal expenditure in the state combined with California's own budget amounts to $100 billion per year; and in addition there are the commercial expenditures represented in Sacramento's "third house," the lobbyists. This huge combined expenditure receives very little media inspection. The financial pages of all the state's newspapers—including the recently expanded business section of the *Los Angeles Times*—are woefully inadequate; while the *Wall Street Journal* (succeeding where the *New York Times* failed) has a large sale with its western edition, this in fact includes little California news. Meanwhile it remains a paradox that in California—the largest state of the leading capitalist nation—the business of government and the government of business receive so little attention from those very profitable businesses, the state's leading television stations and newspapers.

The admirable *California Journal* clearly illustrates how the gap could be filled. This monthly publication provides commendably intelligent and readable coverage. Its own sales success and the fact that many of its articles are written by mem-

6. Quoted in *San Francisco Chronicle* July 20, 1980.

bers of the Sacramento press corps indicate that the inadequate coverage of the state's political economy is due not to the lack of public interest, or to the lack of journalistic ability, but to the parochialism of editors and media managers.

Parochialism is no doubt characteristic of other large states such as Texas, and in New York also the local news largely conforms to retail advertisers' definitions of "local." But it is striking that in such a mobile state as California there should be widespread ignorance; and that in a state with only two major urban areas each should pay so little attention to the other. In the absence of good news coverage, San Francisco and Los Angeles each seems to subscribe to stereotypes of the other which parallel the New York versus California stereotypes.

If the deregulation trend leads to more radio stations in addition to more cable, then there may be a still greater emphasis on California's many localisms.

Localism goes hand in hand with lack of attention to ethnic minorities. The overwhelming thrust of newspapers and television toward the middle-income white suburbs also ignores "minorities," which increasingly in California will not be minorities in terms of population numbers.

The size and probable future political importance of the Hispanic population of California—and its current media invisibility—make it a telling example of a national issue. The Hispanic population must eventually acquire more visibility and more political power. In California especially this must mean more Hispanic media and media electioneering; and both of these in turn will require money and leadership. Sacramento, the California news media, and election campaigning in the state—all these will surely acquire a more bilingual character. The Hispanic impact on the media will occur not only in a few small cities in the Central Valley and in certain suburbs but throughout greater Los Angeles and in the Bay Area.

Will the major television stations and the big suburban newspapers accommodate Hispanics? A block of Hispanic programing, for example, just before the evening's network offerings scarcely accords with the usual station manager's scheduling ideas. Is, then, the alternative more "ghetto programing" and "ghetto newspapers"? Here the history of the American immigrant press of earlier decades might not be repeated; for example, modern telecommunications and the strength of Mexico City itself as a media center mean that Hispanic media in California could for decades to come be supplied not only with Mexico City movies, soap operas, and variety shows but also with Mexico City news.[7] What would be the implications of large numbers of American residents permanently and daily plugged into the culture and politics of a capital city 1500 miles away? We predict that the likely outcome will be mixed: some Anglo media accommodation of Hispanics; and some "conversion" of Hispanics into using Anglo media; and some element of long-term "ghetto" media (partly sustained by the likely continuing two-way movement of population across the U.S.-Mexican border).

In terms of Anglo media "accommodation," a large conundrum concerns how Hollywood will react to discovering that the boundaries of Latin America have been redrawn so as to include Beverly Hills. One site of possible change is the IATSE crafts; also important will be SAG. The existing trend of featuring Latin stars on the screen may shift toward Hispanics. Will Erik Estrada as the vaguely Puerto Rican/Italian/Mexican hero of the California Highway Patrol (in *CHiPs*) be the model? Needless to say, all of this will have to be fought for; it will not come smoothly. The earlier enthusiasm of many Hollywood leaders for Cesar Chavez in the lettuce fields may not carry over into equally enthusiastic support for Hispanic militancy in and around Beverly Hills.

If more Hispanics appear in the output of California-made entertainment programing, perhaps national—United States—perceptions will change. California and its media could educate the rest of the United States: in the future the Hispanics will be the leading minority; with the blacks only second.

California in the Vanguard

California's typicalness of the United States at large means it may be the harbinger of things to come. The gathering

7. The Federal Communications Commission in 1980 launched an investigation to discover whether the corporation which owns KMEX and other television stations is itself foreign owned. *Variety*, September 9, 1980.

strength of newspapers below the "metropolitan" level in the urban areas of the San Francisco Bay and greater Los Angeles is, in this sense, indicative. The possibility of suburban daily papers acquiring readers and strength under enlightened commercial management and imaginative editorial direction is apparent in Long Beach, in the San Fernando Valley, in San Jose, and maybe even in Oakland. Why else would the national newspaper chains have pumped money into them?

Because of its size and electoral strength as a home base, California is bound to be a supplier of national politicians. It also seems safe to predict that California politics—where the polling principle is so uniquely central to the body politic—will continue to be a test market (a pilot episode?) for innovations in both politics and campaign techniques. California history suggests that predicting what policies will surface may be more difficult; however, California may well, as before, seem to move to the right—with some issues and personalities—at the same time as moving to the left with others. It is also easier to predict that California will innovate new media campaign techniques and ways of raising money for media campaigns; it is more difficult to predict whether these will include further variations on the use of musicians to sing the money out of the audiences, or something quite different—such as the political use of cable.

Many things have been claimed for the "new media." Probably not all of these claims will be false. One claim which we expect to be true is that—whatever happens to the hardware—Los Angeles will be the main software provider. We also expect the latest "new Hollywood" of popular music to be linked to the arrival of a wave of sound-cum-video potentates.

California will still be on our minds, and on the minds of our children.

Selected Bibliography

Abrahamsen, David, *Nixon vs. Nixon*, New York: New American Library, 1978.

Andrews, Bart, *The Story of "I Love Lucy,"* New York: Popular Library, 1977.

Baker, Marilyn, *Exclusive! The inside story of Patricia Hearst and the SLA*, New York: Macmillan, 1974.

Balio, Tino (ed.), *The American Film Industry*, Madison: University of Wisconsin Press, 1976.

Banham, Reyner, *Los Angeles: The Architecture of Four Ecologies*, London: Pelican Books, 1973.

Barrett, Marvin (ed.), *Moments of Truth*—The 5th Alfred I. duPont-Columbia University Survey of Broadcast Journalism, New York: T. Crowell, 1975.

Barrett, Rona, *Miss Rona*, New York: Bantam, 1975.

Baxter, John, *The Hollywood Exiles*, London: Macdonald and Janes, 1976.

Bean, Walton, *California: An Interpretive History*, New York, McGraw-Hill, 1978 edition.

Belz, Carl, *The Story of Rock*, New York: Oxford University Press, 1969.

Bernstein, Irving, *The Economics of Television Film Production and Distribution*, Los Angeles: Screen Actors Guild, 1960.

Bollens, John C., and Grant B. Geyer, *Yorty: Politics of a Constant Candidate*, Pacific Palisades, CA: Palisades Publishers, 1973.

Bollens, John C., and G. Robert Williams, *Jerry Brown in a Plain Brown Wrapper*, Pacific Palisades, CA: Palisades Publishers, 1978.

Boyarsky, Bill, *The Rise of Ronald Reagan*, New York: Random House, 1968.

Brenner, Marie, *Going Hollywood*, New York: Dell, 1978.

Brooks, Tim, and Earle Marsh, *The Complete Directory to Prime Time Network TV Shows*, New York: Ballatine, 1979.

Brownlow, Kevin, and John Kobal, *Hollywood: The Pioneers*, London: Collins, 1979.

Brugmann, Bruce (ed.), *The Ultimate Highrise*, San Francisco: Bay Guardian Books, 1971.

Bugliosi, Vincent, and Curt Gentry, *The Manson Murders*, London: The Bodley Head, 1975.

Cannon, Lou, *Reporting: An Inside View*, Sacramento: California Journal Press, 1977.

———, *Ronnie and Jesse: A Political Odyssey*, New York: Doubleday, 1969.

Cantor, Muriel G., *The Hollywood TV Producer*, New York: Basic Books, 1971.

———, *Prime Time Television*, Beverly Hills: Sage Publications, 1980.

Ceplair, Larry, and Steven Englund, *The Inquisition in Hollywood: Politics in the Film Community, 1930–1960*, Garden City, N.Y.: Anchor/Doubleday, 1980.

Chapple, Steve, and Reebee Garofalo, *Rock'n roll Is Here To Pay*, Chicago: Nelson-Hill, 1977.

Cogley, John, *Report on Blacklisting: 1. Movies*, New York: Arno Press & The New York Times, 1972.

Compaine, Benjamin M. (ed.), *Who Owns the Media?* White Plains, N.Y.: Knowledge Industry Publications, 1979.

Conant, Michael, *Anti Trust in the Motion Picture Industry*, Berkeley: University of California Press, 1960.

Cook, Bruce, *The Beat Generation*, New York: Scribner's, 1971.

Costello, William, *The Facts About Nixon*, London: Hutchinson, 1960.

Cowan, Geoffrey, *See No Evil*, New York: Simon and Schuster, 1979.

Delmatier, Royce D, Clarence F. McIntosh, and Earl G. Waters (eds.), *The Rumble of California Politics 1848–1970*, New York: John Wiley, 1970.

Eells, George, *Hedda and Louella*, New York: G. P. Putnam's Sons, 1972.

Fabe, Maxene, *Television Game Shows*, New York: Doubleday, 1979.

Fadiman, William, *Hollywood Now,* London: Thames and Hudson, 1973.

Fawcett, Anthony, *California Rock California Sound,* Los Angeles: Reed Books, 1978.

Gentry, Curt, *The Last Days of the Late, Great State of California,* New York: G.P. Putnam's Sons, 1968.

Gottlieb, Robert and Irene Wolt, *Thinking Big: The Story of the Los Angeles Times,* New York: G.P. Putnam's, 1977.

Halberstam, David, *The Powers That Be,* New York: Knopf, 1979.

Hampton, Benjamin, *History of the American Film Industry from Its Beginnings to 1931,* New York: Dover edition, 1970.

Hardy, Phil, and Dave Laing, *The Encyclopedia of Rock,* Vol. 2, St Albans: Panther Books, 1977.

Harris, Joseph P., *California Politics,* San Francisco: Chandler Publishing, 1967 (Fourth Ed.).

Hart, James D., *A Companion to California,* New York: Oxford University Press, 1978.

Hayward, Brooke, *Haywire,* New York: Knopf, 1977.

Heighton, Elizabeth J., and Don R. Cunningham, *Advertising in the Broadcast Media,* Belmont, CA: Wadsworth, 1976.

Herndon, Booton, *Mary Pickford and Douglas Fairbanks,* New York: W.W. Norton, 1977.

Heston, Charlton, *The Actor's Life: Journals 1956–1976,* New York: Pocket Books, 1979.

Hill, Gladwin, *Dancing Bear. An Inside Look at California Politics,* Cleveland: World Publishing Co., 1968.

James, Marquis, and Bessie Rowland James, *Biography of a Bank: The Story of the Bank of America,* New York: Harper, 1954.

Jarvis, Howard, *I'm Mad as Hell,* New York: Times Books, 1979.

Katcher, Leo, *Earl Warren, A Political Biography,* New York: McGraw-Hill, 1967.

Keogh, James, *President Nixon and the Press,* New York: Funk & Wagnalls, 1972.

Kilduff, Marshall, and Ron Javers, *The Suicide Cult,* New York: Bantam Books, 1978.

Krieger, Susan, *Hip Capitalism,* Beverly Hills: Sage Publications, 1979.

League of Women Voters of California, *A Guide to California Government,* 1977 edition.

Leary, Mary Ellen, *Phantom Politics. Campaigning in California,* Washington, D.C.: Public Affairs Press, 1977.

Lewis, Joseph, *What Makes Reagan Run: A Political Profile,* New York: McGraw-Hill, 1968.

Longstreet, Stephen, *All Star Cast: An Anecdotal History of Los Angeles,* New York: T. Y. Crowell, 1977.

Lorenz, J.D., *Jerry Brown: The Man on the White Horse,* Boston: Houghton Mifflin, 1978.

Lyle, Jack, *The News in Megalopolis,* San Francisco: Chandler Publishing, 1967.

McFadden, Cyra, *The Serial. A Year in the Life of Marin County,* New York: Knopf, 1977.

MacShane, Frank, *The Life of Raymond Chandler,* New York: Dutton, 1976.

McWilliams, Carey, *California: The Great Exception,* Westport, Conn.: Greenwood Press, 1971. First published in 1949.

———— (ed.), *The California Revolution,* New York: Grossman Publishers, 1968.

Mankiewicz, Frank, *Perfectly Clear. Nixon from Whittier to Watergate,* New York: Quadrangle/N.Y. Times Book Co., 1973.

Mazlish, Bruce, *In Search of Nixon,* New York: Basic Books, 1972.

Medved, Michael, and David Wallechinsky, *What Really Happened to the Class of '65?* New York: Random House, 1976.

Meister, Dick, and Anne Loftis, *A Long Time Coming: The Struggle to Unionize America's Farm Workers,* New York: Macmillan, 1977.

Monaco, James, *American Film Now,* New York: Oxford University Press, 1979.

Morgan, Neil, *The California Syndrome,* New York: Ballantine Books, 1971.

Murphy, George (with Victor Lasky) *Say . . . didn't you used to be George Murphy?* Bartholomew House, 1970.

Nadeau, Remi, *California: The New Society,* New York: David McKay, 1963.

Newcomb, Horace, *TV: The Most Popular Art,* Garden City, N.Y.: Anchor Press/Doubleday, 1974.

Nixon, Richard M., *Six Crises,* New York: Doubleday, 1962.

Owen, Bruce M., *Economics and Freedom of Expression,* Cambridge, Mass.: Ballinger, 1975.

Pack, Robert, *Jerry Brown: The Philosopher Prince,* New York: Stein & Day, 1978.

Parsons, Louella O., *Tell It to Louella,* New York: G.P. Putnam's Sons, 1961.

Powdermaker, Hortense, *Hollywood: The Dream Factory,* London: Secker and Warburg, 1951.

Powers, Ron, *The Newscasters,* New York: St Martin's Press, 1977.

Pye, Michael, and Lynda Miles, *The Movie Brats,* New York: Holt, Rinehart and Winston, 1979.

Rather, Dan, and Gary Paul Gates, *The Palace Guard,* New York: Warner Books, 1975.

Reagan, Ronald, and Richard G. Hubler, *Where's the Rest of Me?* New York: Duell, Sloan and Pearce, 1965.

Rivers, William L., and David M. Rubin, *A Region's Press: Anatomy of Newspapers in the San Francisco Bay Area,* Berkeley: Univ. of California Institute of Governmental Studies, 1971.

Rosow, Eugene, *Born To Lose: The Gangster Film in America,* New York: Oxford University Press, 1978.

Ross, Murray, *Stars and Strikes: Unionization of Hollywood,* New York: Columbia University Press, 1941.

Rosten, Leo C., *Hollywood: The Movie Colony, the Movie Makers,* New York: Harcourt Brace, 1941.

Salzman, Ed, *Jerry Brown: High Priest and Low Politician,* Sacramento: California Journal Press, 1976.

Schary, Dore, *Heyday,* Boston: Little Brown, 1979.

Schell, Orville, *Brown,* New York: Random House, 1978.

Schickel, Richard, *His Picture in the Papers,* New York: Charterhouse, 1973.

———, *The Disney Version. The Life, Times, Art and Commerce of Walt Disney,* New York: Simon and Schuster, 1968.

Shanks, Bob, *The Cool Fire: How To Make It in Television,* New York: Vintage, 1977.

Shaw, Arnold, *The Rock Revolution,* New York: Crowell-Collier Press, 1969.

Shaw, David, *Journalism Today,* New York: Harper's College Press, 1977.

Spitz, Robert S., *The Making of Superstars,* New York: Doubleday, 1978.

Stein, Ben, *The View from Sunset Boulevard,* New York: Basic Books, 1979.

Sterling, Christopher H., and Timothy R. Haight, *The Mass Media: Aspen Institute Guide to Communication Industry Trends,* New York: Praeger, 1978.

Stokes, Geoffrey, *Star-making Machinery,* New York: Random House, 1977.

Swanberg, W.A., *Citizen Hearst,* New York: Bantam Books, 1963.

Swanson, Walter S.J., *The Thin Gold Watch. A Personal History of the Newspaper Copleys,* New York: Macmillan, 1964.

Tebbel, John, *The Life and Good Times of William Randolph Hearst,* New York: Dutton, 1952.

Thompson, Hunter, *Hell's Angels, "A strange and terrible saga,"* New York: Ballantine, 1966.

Tynan, Kenneth, *Show People,* New York: Simon and Schuster, 1979.

Wagner, Walter, *Beverly Hills: Inside the Golden Ghetto,* New York: Grosset and Dunlap, 1976.

Wale, Michael, *Voxpop: Profiles of the Pop Process,* London: Harrap, 1972.

Westmore, Frank, and Muriel Davidson, *The Westmores of Hollywood,* Philadelphia: Lippincott, 1976.

Wills, Garry, *Nixon Agonistes: The Crisis of the Self-Made Man,* New York: New American Library, 1971.

Wirt, Frederick M., *Power in the City. Decision Making in San Francisco,* Berkeley: University of California Press, 1974.

Wolper, David L., and Quincy Troupe, *The Inside Story of TV's "Roots",* New York: Warner, 1978.

Zheutlin, Barbara, and David Talbot, *Creative Differences: Profiles of Hollywood Dissidents,* Boston: South End Press, 1978.